THE THIRD GENERATION

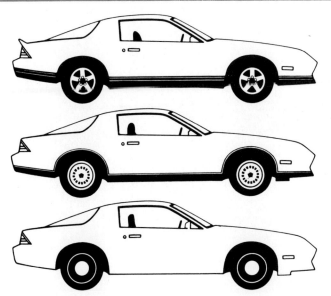

by Michael Lamm

Please note: This book was researched and written between February and October, 1981. Some of the information and photos therefore reflect pre-production models. Any discrepancies between prototypes and production cars will be corrected in updated editions of Camaro, The Third Generation.
—The Publisher

For Rob

First printing, December 1981

ISBN 0-932128-02-5

Library of Congress Card Catalog Number 81-90577

Lamm-Morada Publishing Co. Inc.
Post Office Box 7607
Stockton, California 95207

CONTENTS

Chapter One
Starting with a Clean Sheet
The Third-Generation Camaro Takes Shape

Advanced design executive Dave Holls (right) and designer Bill Porter admire Roger Hughet's glass-roofed model that set third-generation F-Car's theme.

"CONSIDER THE SUCCESS of the previous Camaro and Firebird," says assistant executive designer Stan Wilen. "Here were two cars whose success is now legendary. What, then, do we do next?

"Should we create a new car purely in the image of the old? Has the Camaro driver become more sophisticated? Should the car again reflect its uniquely American roots? What have we learned from European design? Should the new Camaro and Firebird reflect a kind of elegance—or should it update its image of pure power? How big should it be? How can we make it do more? How total the commitment to aero?

"We went through some rigorous philosophical soul searching to find the right blend...to make the new F-Car as relevant today as the second generation was in 1970. The last Camaro ran for 12 years, so we had some interesting debates. The initial instincts of many of us were to repeat our past successes. Success makes cowards of us. It's easy to try something new if you don't have a winner, but we *had* a winner, and it's always difficult to cut loose from something that's doing well.

"The new Camaro and Firebird," concludes Wilen, "are very different from the previous generation, yet their heritage is clear to see. We didn't abandon tradition. We just made the car more relevant and better-looking."

Every new automobile starts with a few quick lines on paper. Wherever the design goes after that—into File 13 or through innumerable further sketches and tape drawings, scale models and full-sized clays, interior bucks, engine bucks, trunk bucks, into

and out of a dozen computer programs, through product clinics, component cars, pre-prototypes, prototypes, die models, steel dies, pilot assembly, and finally down a production line—the seed for Job One came from that first drawing.

F-Cars are Camaros and Firebirds. They've been called that since their inception in model year 1967. From that day to this, Chevrolet and Pontiac F-Cars have shared all major inner and many outer body panels plus chassis components and, at various times, engines.

In their earliest stages, all F-Cars were and are developed side by side. That means you can't really talk about the Camaro without including some history of the Firebird as well.

Advanced drawings for the third-generation F-Car sprang from an advanced studio deep inside the General Motors Design Center in Warren, Mich., just north of Detroit. At that time, the program was destined to become an all-new 1980 Camaro and Firebird, not an '82 model. In mid-1975, in GM's Advanced One studio, William L. (Bill) Porter, his one assistant and two designers began turning out very preliminary 1980 F-Car sketches.

"In July of 1975," recalls Bill Porter, "we started working on proposals for an entirely new F-Car. At that time we had no idea what the next-generation Camaro and Firebird was going to be like, so we looked at rear-engined proposals, mid-engined pro-

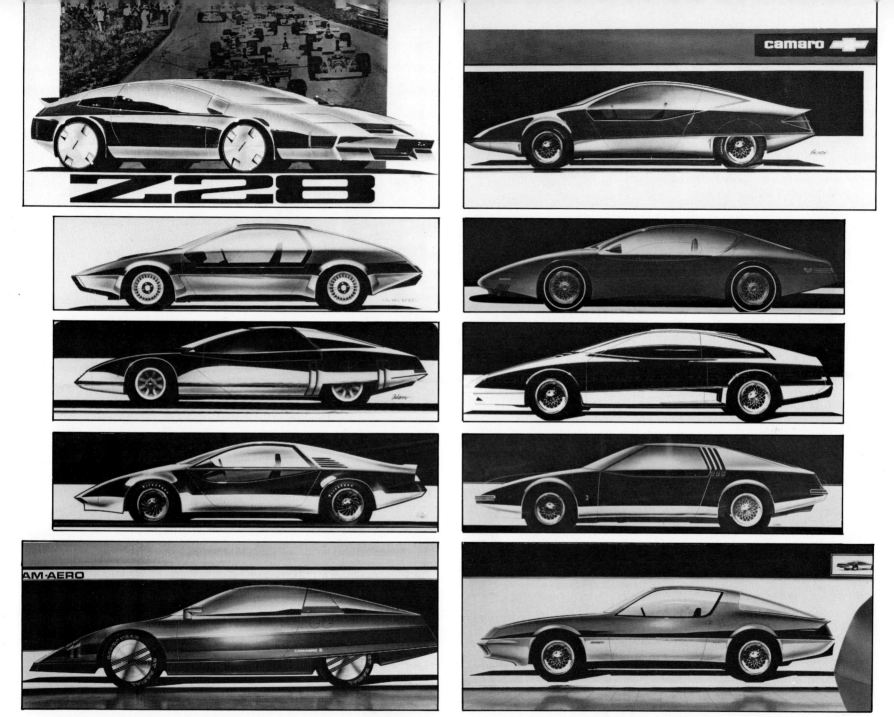

Because designers didn't know at first whether all-new Camaro would end up with front-wheel drive, rear drive, or mid engine, early drawings proposed all possibilities. These sketches represent a tiny fraction of the ideas generated by Jerry Palmer's Chevy Three production studio and Bill Porter's Advanced One.

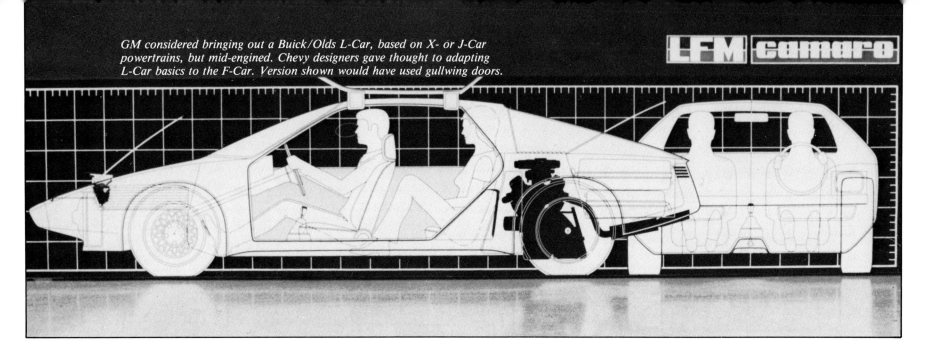

GM considered bringing out a Buick/Olds L-Car, based on X- or J-Car powertrains, but mid-engined. Chevy designers gave thought to adapting L-Car basics to the F-Car. Version shown would have used gullwing doors.

posals, conventional layouts, and ultimately at proposals that involved front-wheel drive [fwd] with transverse engines as in the X-Car.''

Talk persisted for quite some time—especially in planning and management circles—that the coming F-Car might share the X-Car's body plan and the X's basic powertrains. Some voices spoke out for fwd on the grounds of F/X component interchangeability. General Motors Engineering Staff went so far as to propose and build a concept car that put the X-Car's transverse power unit behind the driver's seat—with rear-wheel drive—for a mid-engined layout.

And although the mid-engined proposals fell by the wayside fairly soon due to packaging restrictions (not enough room for four people), the front-versus-rear-drive controversy continued right up until 1978. Nor was the final decision made lightly, because $1.5 *billion* rode on the outcome!

In mid-1975, though, there was no big rush to decide. Then-current Camaros and Firebirds were doubling and redoubling sales every season. No one could have predicted back then that the second-generation F-Cars would enjoy such an amazingly long life: a 12-year run, far longer than GM's normal 3-4-year body cycles. Yet everyone realized that the second generation couldn't last forever and that a replacement would eventually have to be found.

This long leadtime gave Design Staff a chance to put its best efforts into the upcoming third-generation Camaros and Firebirds. ''The program was unusual in this regard,'' observes GM design director Charles M. (Chuck) Jordan. ''We all felt strongly about doing a new F-Car. The second generation had been going so well for so long that we wanted to do the third generation very, very carefully. We all love that car. This is an automobile you feel; something you *want* to drive. And because the second generation wore so well, we felt a responsibility to do another very careful job, and that's one reason we got started early in Bill's advanced studio.''

Bill Porter had been *the* man behind the clean, sleek lines of the second-generation Firebird—the car that came out on Feb. 26, 1970. He'd also refined the blue-stripes-on-white paint scheme for the 1969 and 1970½ Trans Ams. In 1972, Porter left Pontiac to become chief designer of GM's Advanced Studio One, a position he held until mid-1979. His assistant was Roger E. Hughet, and the Advanced One team included senior designers Elia (Russ) Russinoff and David S. McIntosh, with Orval C. Selders as

During the 1975-77 period, one recurring early theme involved oval side glass with a dipped beltline, severely raked windshield, and tight wheel cutouts.

studio engineer. Davis Rossi was chief modeler, his assistant being Harold Chyz (pronounced *Chick*).

Overseeing this design group—plus all other GM advanced studios—was David R. Holls, executive designer in charge of General Motors' advanced and international auto design. Holls oversaw Porter's studio and the F-Car's progress on a personal, day-to-day basis.

As mentioned, the initial projected release date for an all-new F-Car was 1980, not 1982. In those very early stages, there had been no set package to work from—no specific measurements such as wheelbase, overall length, weight, or even engine placement. And to make the job even more challenging, GM at that time was contemplating bringing out what it called the L-Car.

The L-Car, originally also intended for 1980 introduction, would have been a small, sporty 4-seater from Buick and Oldsmobile. Had it come to pass, the L-Car would have been based on either X-Car or J-Car fwd components. Its dimensions, in inches, were: wheelbase 102.5, overall length 187.7, and overall width 66.6. The question quite

Strong attempts were made to integrate or blend in front and rear bumpers. Narrow pillars and flush-fitting glass led way eventually to Roger Hughet's

theme model, especially with its emphasis on glass. Advanced designers worked for many months without benefit of a "package" or dimensional specifications.

Aerodynamics remained uppermost in designers' minds, leading to Citroen-like renditions (left), sharply pointed noses and tails. Hatchbacks were being

considered very early, as were patch mirrors, faired-in airdams, plus bold fender flares. These elements, though, hadn't yet led to an acceptable theme.

naturally arose, Can a third-generation F-Car be carved from—or built in conjunction with—the Buick/Olds L-Car?

Orval Selders comments, "In those early stages, we had at least two versions going all the time—front drive and rear drive. You have a different wheel location with fwd—shorter dash-to-axle distance. When we'd do a model, one side would be front-wheel drive and the other side was conventional. We were also doing a third version in the very initial stages. I don't think [anyone] took it too seriously, but we talked about a mid-engined version. There were a number of scale models done, which we stored here in Advanced One."

In the autumn of 1976, the engineering people entered the F-Car picture. Engineers from Chevrolet, Pontiac, and GM's central engineering staff were assigned the task of defining what the next generation of Camaros and Firebirds should be.

Divisional and corporate engineers worked independently that fall and, in late Nov. 1976, Chevrolet took the lead by establishing an F-Car task force, based inside the Fisher Body Div. office building at the GM Technical Center. The effort at this point was to home in on body dimensions.

Two weeks later, in a further move to pool talents and combine ideas from Chevrolet, Pontiac, Engineering Staff, and Design Staff, an F-Car Advanced Project Center was formed within the Design Staff body development room.

Project Centers consist basically of groups of planners, engineers, designers, cost analysts, and so forth, brought together from various divisions and staffs, housed under one roof, all working on one car or one specific project, their main function being to coordinate and make sure that what needs to be done gets done. We'll talk more about Project Centers in Chapter Three, but an *Advanced* Project Center, which this was at the time, is charged with doing initial explorations aimed at laying the groundwork for a full-fledged Project Center.

At this very early point, the F-Car Advanced Project Center consisted of only three people. Representing Chevrolet Engineering was chassis engineer Robert J. (Bob) Haglund, who held a master's degree in engineering from the Illinois Institute of Technology and who'd been an active member of the Project Center responsible for GM's first downsized automobile, the 1977 B-Car.

Pontiac was at first represented by Duane F. Miller, who soon left to become director of engineering for Volkswagen of America. His place was taken by Robert H. (Bob)

While work continued upstairs in Palmer's Camaro production studio, Porter, Palmer, and Schinella joined forces within Advanced One downstairs and tried in vain to arrive at an F-Car theme together.

Knickerbocker, a 26-year veteran of Pontiac. Knickerbocker later became head of the full-blown F-Car Project Center.

Design Staff sent engineer/designer Hulki Aldikacti, who eventually went on to head Pontiac's P-Car Project Center. Working with designers in Advanced One as well as those in Chevrolet's production Studio Three and Pontiac's Studio Two, the struggle now began in earnest to sort out a direction and thus dimensions plus a personality for the future F-Car.

On Jan. 24, 1977, at a special evening meeting in the Design Staff auditorium, the Advanced Project Center group made a presentation to divisional and corporate heads. This presentation put forth not one but three possible plans: 1) a new F-Car based on the upcoming fwd X-Car, 2) an F-Car based on the rear-wheel-drive (rwd) A-Car, and 3) an F-Car with midship engine placement, also based on X-Car components. Sketches and clay models were shown along with projections of costs, fuel economy, handling, straight-line performance, packaging, and the anticipated market for smaller cars.

Based on this presentation, the assembled General Motors executives took an informal vote and approved the F/A-Car concept. In other words, they suggested that the future F-Car be based essentially on A-Car components—that it remain front-engined and rear-wheel drive.

This idea, they realized, needed further exploration, but the exploration, they felt, should head in the F/A-Car direction, with the outcome leading to further evaluation by GM's powerful Product Policy Group. The Product Policy Group would take up the matter in Oct. 1977, or in eight months' time.

Design Staff now seemed to have a direction and an approximate size for the F-Car. Bill Porter's advanced design group and Jerry Palmer's Chevy Three studio began concentrating on conventional F-Car drivetrain layouts and thus temporarily shelved fwd and mid-engined configurations.

Now a number of important points need to be made at this juncture, I feel, and although they'll crop up again in our chapter on engineering, they can't be ignored when talking about the new F-Car's design evolution.

First of all, some automotive writers and even a few Camaro enthusiasts have expressed dismay that the third-generation F-Car "ignored" or "overlooked" front-wheel drive; that designers and planners of the 1982 Camaro clung to "old-fashioned," "outmoded," or "conventional" engineering simply because of the success of the previous F-Cars.

Nothing could be further from the truth. We'll examine the fwd/rwd question more thoroughly in our engineering chapter, but briefly, the front-engine/rear-drive decision

GM Body Designations

As of 1981, General Motors produced 11 basic bodies and marketed them under 34 individual nameplates. Since GM engineers and designers often refer to body-letter codes rather than specific makes and models, here's a reference table. Keep in mind, though, that these were designations used in model-years 1980-81, and names do change with time.

	Chevrolet	Pontiac	Oldsmobile	Buick	Cadillac
A-Cars	Malibu	Le Mans	Cutlass	Century	—
A-Spl*	Monte Carlo	Grand Prix	Cutlass Supreme	Regal	—
B-Cars	Impala, Caprice	Catalina, Bonnev'l	Delta 88	LeSabre	—
C-Cars	—	—	Olds 98	Electra	Cpe de Ville Fleetwood
E-Cars	—	—	Toronado	Riviera	Eldorado
F-Cars	Camaro	Firebird	—	—	—
H-Spl	Monza	Sunbird	Starfire	Skyhawk	—
J-Cars	Cavalier	J2000	—	—	Cimarron
K-Cars	—	—	—	—	Seville
T-Cars	Chevette	T1000	—	—	—
X-Cars	Citation	Phoenix	Omega	Skylark	—
Y-Cars	Corvette	—	—	—	—

*A-Specials are sometimes called G-Cars.

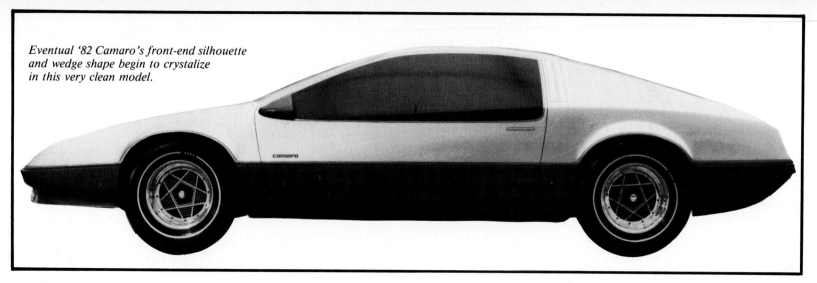

Eventual '82 Camaro's front-end silhouette and wedge shape begin to crystalize in this very clean model.

meant, in many ways, getting the best performance and handling from a car intended to excel in those areas.

In a nutshell, the three major reasons leading GM to decide on front-engine/rear-drive for the 1982 Camaro were these: 1) better cornering, 2) more equal weight distribution, and 3) greater flexibility in the choice of engines.

I don't mean to belabor these engineering considerations in a chapter on design, but I'd like to spend a few paragraphs here to explain.

Regarding handling, in a fwd car both traction and steering are done by the front tires. It's easy enough to show—and I've given illustrations in Chapter Three—that when you combine these functions on one axle, both functions tend to lose potency. In other words, tires that give a certain percentage of their effort to propelling a car can't contribute 100% to steering or making it corner.

A rear-drive vehicle, however, in which the front tires steer and the rears push, splits these two functions and gives all four tires more effectiveness in each duty.

On the point of weight distribution, it's obvious enough that a fwd car, with its engine and transaxle directly over the front wheels, puts the major weight bias forward. GM's fwd X-Car 2-door hatchback, for example, has a weight distribution of 64/36. This means the front axle carries 64% of the car's total weight; the real axle 36%. Compare this with the 1982 Z-28's weight distribution of 55/45 and the 4-cylinder Camaro's of 51/49.

As for engine flexibility, one of the primary questions early in the F-Car program was, Shall we include a V-8? With fwd and the confines of the projected F/X-, F/L-, or F/J-Car's transverse engine mounting, a V-8 was out of the question. There simply wasn't room in a fwd F-Car. And a V-6, even turbocharged and supertuned, didn't seem to have the muscle nor the relatively understressed longevity of a bigger V-8.

There were many, many other factors that finally combined to make the third-generation Camaro "conventional" in its drivetrain layout. As I say, I'll hit those reasons a lot harder in the appropriate chapter. But I don't want you to feel—as some people still do—that Chevrolet and GM didn't explore fwd or have good reasons for going front-engine/rear-drive.

Yet as you'll see in a moment, the fwd/rwd controversy wasn't dead by any means; in fact quite the opposite. And while the advanced designers and engineers enjoyed a few months of F/A-Car direction, that era came to an abrupt end with the first corporate Future Product Conference, held on May 9, 1977.

General Motors' worldwide product planning staff hosted the Future Product Conference, an idea conceived by GM president Elliott M. (Pete) Estes. Estes called this large meeting of some 100 people to sort out and plan for the federal govern-

ment's 1980-85 CAFE (corporate average fuel economy) requirements. CAFE fleet averages at that time called for 27.5 mpg by 1985, with interim mpg targets increasing to that figure year by year.

The CAFE edict hit all U.S. automakers like a ton of bricks. The question: How are we going to do it? GM's answer could come only through judicious, detailed, corporate-wide planning.

To make a long story short, the May 9 Future Product Conference concluded with an accelerated downsizing program for all of GM's car lines. The plan called for the creation of a small *front-wheel-drive* F-Car for 1980/82. This was now to be based on X-Car or J-Car components.

What this new fwd recommendation did was to throw all the advanced designers' rwd sketches and clay models out the window and the Advanced Project Center engineers into turmoil. Design Staff, meanwhile, slowed to a snail's pace in its search for a new F-Car. Porter, Palmer, and their studios were waiting not only for firmer fwd/rwd direction, but they looked toward an uncertain future pending the fast-approaching retirement of William L. Mitchell, the staff's vice president of 19 years. No one knew who would take Mitchell's place nor what his replacement might want in terms of a future F-Car.

Throughout the summer and fall of 1977, the F-Car Advanced Project Center got down to the business of studying and re-examining the handling potential of fwd cars.

Under Chevrolet's chief vehicles engineer Tom Zimmer, a handling group headed by Fred Schaafsma tried valiantly to get several fwd automobiles to handle in ways consistent with standards set for the new Camaro Z-28. A similar team at Pontiac, led by Norm Fugate, was trying to do the same thing: make a small fwd car handle to the expectations of Trans Am buyers. That's another story for Chapter Three, but briefly, no fwd car—stock, modified, or cobbled—ever met the handling targets set for the F-Car by Chevrolet and Pontiac engineers.

In addition to gathering handling and performance data, the Advanced Project Center staff spent that 1977 summer and autumn weighing other relative merits of fwd versus rwd—aspects like cost, mass (weight), fuel efficiency, and packaging. It's true that a fwd F/X-Car or F/J-Car could be made smaller, lighter, and thus more economical without generally decreasing passenger and cargo capacity. But it's also true that handling and performance would suffer in a fwd F-Car.

One more bit of history—an ironic twist—needs to be mentioned at this point. It's the final factor in the F-Car's move away from fwd, and it shows how quickly world events

Done originally in Oct. 1976 as a fwd Firebird, Hughet's low, rakish, glass-domed model was banished to a warehouse when rwd came in.   Dave Holls...

can change the shape, size, and configuration of an automobile. I'll let Chevrolet chassis engineer Bob Haglund explain.

"You have to go back to the way GM cars were selling in 1977," Haglund reminds us. "We'd just launched our 1977 B-Car—GM's first downsized car—and it immediately became one of the most successful sellers we'd ever built. Nineteen seventy-seven was just a terrific year. Then in 1978 we downsized our A-Cars—our intermediates—and 1978 also turned out to be a great year.

"All those sales of relatively large A-, B-, and C-Cars, though, had a dark side for our planners, because when they projected sales out toward 1985, the 27.5-mpg CAFE target looked pretty impossible.

"We who'd been interested in handling," continues Haglund, "had always wanted a rear-drive Camaro, but for a little while there in '77, a large segment of planning opinion said we ought to make the new F-Car front-wheel drive, because that would be better for corporate fuel economy.

"Then the bottom fell out of the big-car market. Gasoline prices kept racing upward, and events in the Middle East had people worried whether oil would be available at *any*

price. Interest rates soared, as did new-car prices, and GM's volume estimators finally decided that the switch to small cars was permanent. By that time small cars were selling like crazy. And suddenly we here at General Motors weren't worried about the 27.5-mpg future anymore. In fact, Pete Estes told reporters before he retired that he thought GM could look for 31.0 mpg by 1985."

This fact—that Americans voluntarily switched to more fuel-efficient, smaller cars—allowed General Motors to rethink the F-Car question. A mini F was no longer so desperately needed to meet the 27.5-mpg standard. Thus the arguments in favor of rear drive for the F-Car prevailed a second time.

A nd while all this back-and-forth, fwd-versus-rwd was going on, Design Staff was doing its best to keep in step. The shuffle was taking a toll, though, and enthusiasm for the F-Car program seemed to be dwindling inside both Bill Porter's advanced studio and Jerry Palmer's Chevy Three production studio.

The other vital factor that entered during the first half of 1977 was everyone's realiza-

...remembered it, called it back, and convinced management to instate Hughet's model as the F-Car theme. Painting above now hangs in Chuck Jordan's office.

tion that Design Staff vice president William L. (Bill) Mitchell would retire on July 31. This added another measure of uncertainty to an already clouded F-Car future, because Mr. Mitchell didn't want to saddle his successor with a completed design that might not turn out to be appropriate.

So, as I mentioned, progress on designing an all-new F-Car came almost to a standstill during the early part of 1977. It was at this point that the corporation decided not to aim toward a 1980 introduction date but rather, since second-generation Camaros and Firebirds were still selling well, to postpone the new car until 1982.

Bill Mitchell's successor became Irvin W. (Irv) Rybicki, who took office as vice president in charge of GM's Design Staff on Aug. 1, 1977. One of Mr. Rybicki's first acts was to revitalize the F-Car program. Two weeks after he came into his new position, Rybicki ordered Palmer and Porter to roll their best full-sized clay models into the viewing yard outside the Design Staff auditorium. On hand at this event—in addition to Rybicki, Palmer, and Porter—were design director Chuck Jordan, design executive of all advanced studios David R. Holls, design executive of all production studios Jack Humbert, and assistant executive designers Stanley R. Wilen and Edward R. Taylor.

Although he hadn't been directly involved with the F-Car previously, Mr. Rybicki had watched that struggle at a distance. "I'd been associated with Olds, Buick, and Cadillac," recounts Rybicki, "but I had on occasion seen what was developing with the F-Cars, and one of the first decisions I made as vice president was to move Bill Porter's and Jerry Palmer's models into the viewing yard.

"At that time, the 1980 program had gone toward cars with large rear quarter windows, like the new J-Car fastback coupe and the Toyota Celica liftback. The rule that I laid on the chaps at that viewing was that the 1982 F-Car would have 1-piece sideglass, period; no quarter windows. Like the second-generation F-Car. I wanted the '82-model Camaro and Firebird to be associated more with the Corvette than anything else.

"Also," concludes Irv Rybicki, "the earlier clay models had hard edges in their roofs, quarter panels, and front fenders, and I stopped all that on that day, too. The car would be softer in character, but certainly not as soft as the previous model, because the new package was so much smaller.... That really started the development of the 1982 Camaro as it was released. And it all began that day in the viewing yard."

In late 1977, with F-Car theme set, GM Design Staff began the job of productionizing Hughet's model. Styrofoam armature formed core of full-sized clay.

By Jan. 24, 1978, GM gave rwd final okay. Design Staff now had a deadline to meet. Roger Hughet (right) helped transform his theme into a workable car.

Despite the stops and starts, Bill Porter feels his advanced design group contributed something very valuable to the eventual '82 design. "Vehicles like ours become a framework on which to hang new ideas," he explains. "In my opinion, perhaps the most important role for an advanced studio is to explore new ideas—ideas you might bank for a while. You can always draw on them later. Some never earn interest, but others do."

One that did was a front-wheel-drive model, conceived back in Oct. 1976 by Porter's assistant, Roger Hughet. This model set the theme—the *religion*, as Chuck Jordan calls it—for what ultimately became the 1982 Firebird and, less directly, the '82 Camaro.

Hughet's ⅓-scale model had a long, flowing upper—a roof entirely covered with glass. Underneath the glass stood a conventional steel roof, supported on normal though slender pillars. You could see the roof and pillars through the glass.

Not only was Hughet's use of glass unusual, but the way the glass cascaded down off the roof and then flowed outward at its bottom edges—this, too, stood out as an especially attractive design notion.

Roger's model, originally done as a fwd car and painstakingly modeled by design sculptor Stan Szczepanek (pronounced *Sipanek*), stood on display in the studio throughout the early part of 1977. When word came down, though, that fwd was out and rwd was in, Hughet's glass-domed silver model, being fwd, was packed off to a Design Center warehouse along with other now-obsolete contenders. However, during its long stay in Advanced One, Hughet had made several renderings of the glass-topped car, including the traditional full-sized airbrush side view and a high-angle portrait. This portrait hung—and still hangs—in Chuck Jordan's office. We'll see in a moment how Hughet's model came to influence the '82 F-Car, but before that, I'd like to jump ahead a little.

On Dec. 20, 1977, GM's top management—including board chairman Thomas A. Murphy, president Elliott M. Estes, technical vice president Howard H. Kehrl, North American automotive vice president F. James McDonald, and financial vice president Roger B. Smith—made it official. They met in Pete Estes' office on the 14th floor of the General Motors building in downtown Detroit specifically to talk about the F-Car fwd/rwd dilemma.

Based on recommendations and presentations that had been made mostly by divisional engineers during the previous several months, these men decided once and for all that the 1982 Camaro and Firebird *should* go rear-wheel drive. About a month later, on Jan. 24, 1978, the Product Policy Group likewise endorsed the rwd 1982 F-Car but took away the stipulation that it had to be based on A-Car components. A direction for the 1982 F-Car had been set at last.

But when rwd was reinstated, a deadline arrived with it. Dec. 11, 1978 became the target for final management approval of a full-sized 1982 Camaro clay. That date, when announced, loomed just over a year away.

By late 1977, not one but three separate design studios got seriously involved in doing new 1982 F-Car proposals: Bill Porter's Advanced One plus Jerry Palmer's Chevy Three and John Schinella's Pontiac Two production studios. All worked independently for a time, trying to come up with a theme for the 1982 Camaro and Firebird.

It soon became apparent, though, that these separate efforts weren't bearing fruit. So the three studio chiefs—Porter, Palmer, and Schinella—met with Design Staff management and decided to pool talents. Designers from Chevy Three and Pontiac Two would continue their independent pursuits upstairs but would also participate in a group effort in Advanced One downstairs. Thus for several months, both before and after the rwd decisions, Jerry Palmer and John Schinella plus members of their staffs spent time in the confines of Advanced One.

"We had two platforms in the studio," remembers Bill Porter, "and the Firebird and Camaro tracked parallel. It was a nice arrangement, although it did tend to be a little crowded." Unfortunately, this cooperative effort also came to naught.

It was at this point, late in 1977, that Dave Holls remembered Roger Hughet's glass-roofed fwd model in the warehouse.

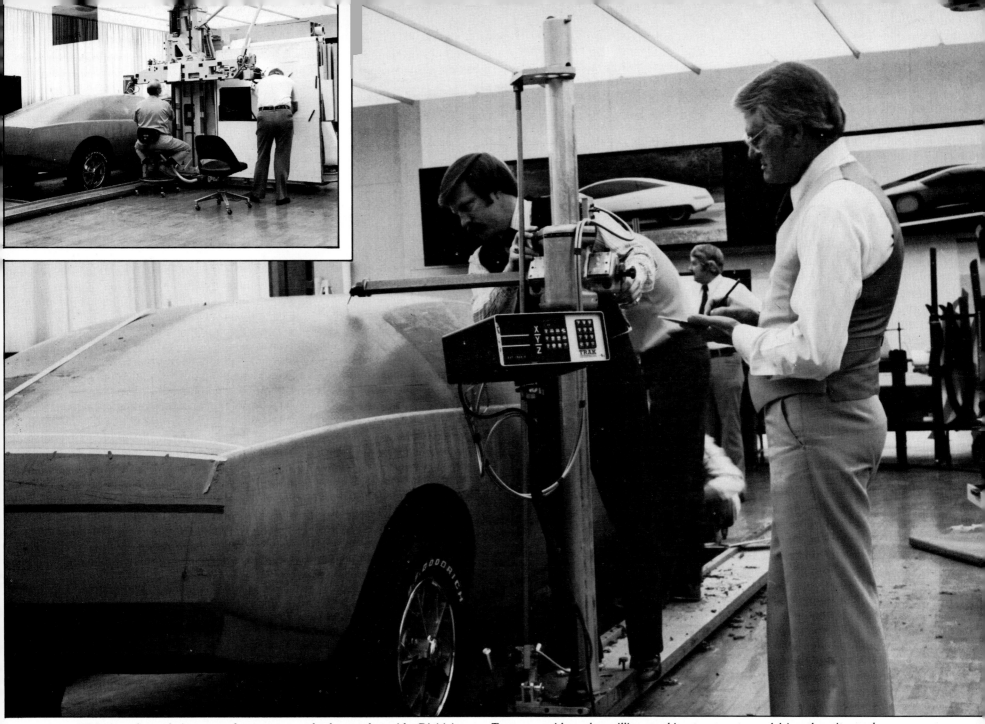

With time short, designers used computers and other modern aids. Digitizing electronic surface recorder (inset) makes tape of the clay's three dimensions.

Tape can guide a clay-milling machine to recreate model in other sites and sizes. Manual point taker with digital readout assures side-to-side accuracy.

Hughet's theme model worked well full size.   Palmer's Chevy Three production studio released the upper, which remained amazingly faithful to original.

"Roger's model and sketches set the whole theme for the 1982 car," says Holls as he looks back on pulling the model back out of storage. "The way the upper is handled; then the line that comes from the wedge shape over the front wheels...that and the upper, those are it! That's the whole theme."

The totally glass-encased roof wouldn't be practical for production, of course, but one of the striking facets of Hughet's design could easily be translated into a large, intricately shaped "backlight" or rear window. The usable aspect of Hughet's glass roof was the rear window's cascading flow—its compound-curved lower edging where it meets the main body section.

In explaining this huge piece of glass as finally produced, Bill Porter suggests, "Think of it as the back of a violin or cello. It flares outward in all directions at the bottom—goes from convex in the middle to concave all around the edges. So it has that wonderful stretched quality. It's beautiful but very, very hard to form."

Chuck Jordan unhesitatingly endorses Hughet as the man behind the 1982 F-Car theme. But credit must also go to Dave Holls for recognizing the merits of Hughet's design, for bringing it back from exile, and for championing it at just the right moment.

Nor would Hughet's concept have gotten far without enthusiastic support from designers of the stature of Irv Rybicki, Chuck Jordan, Jack Humbert, Ed Taylor, Stan Wilen, Jerry Palmer, and John Schinella. In the advanced area, inspiration and discussion flowed from Dave Holls through his assistant executive, Bernie Smith, to Porter and Hughet. The 1982 Camaro and Firebird mark one of the highest recent expressions of design team effort—an effort, by the way, that was just then—in late 1977—beginning to go together.

Roger Hughet's model set the theme, but it now had to be groomed and sweetened to turn it into a real-world car. That became the job of the production studios: Palmer's Chevy Three and Schinella's Pontiac Two.

"When we got to this stage—the production-studio stage," recalls Jerry Palmer, "Schinella and I worked very closely. We worked closely *to stay different!*"

John Schinella concurs. "Jerry and I shook hands and said, Hey, we want two different, unique vehicles." But because Schinella and his staff still had some finishing touches to put on the Pontiac J2000, initial productionizing of the '82 Firebird remained in the hands of Porter and Hughet.

Palmer's Chevy Three staff got to work on the 1982 Camaro immediately and became, in effect, the lead studio. The F-Car's 62-degree windshield, its roof, the huge glass liftback, and the doors were all released from Palmer's studio. Those remain—to this day—the only outer body panels common to both cars.

Palmer's assistant in Chevy Three was Ted Schroeder, a Formula Vee racer and a designer who'd contributed heavily to previous Camaros. Schroeder also provided dozens of advanced sketches and studies for the third generation. Senior designer Randy Wittine likewise constituted an important member of Palmer's team. Wittine had long worked with Camaro race-car builder Roger Penske and still, in fact, works with him. Randy also provided the graphics for all the IROC Camaros, the IMSA Monzas, and several competition Corvettes.

John Cafaro and John Adams also contributed mightily to the Chevy Three effort, as did studio chief engineer George McLean and chief modeler Al Tholl. Tholl, in fact, had modeled all Corvettes since 1964 and all Camaros since '67. These, then, became

John Schinella's production studio took theme more directly into the Firebird, retaining hidden headlamps and more of the original model's overall shape.

One of Irv Rybicki's first acts as new GM vice president was to view full-sized models. Rybicki mandated elimination of small quarter panes behind doors.

the key studio people responsible for shaping the third generation in its final form.

Several specific items on the '82 F-Car took considerably more work to refine than normal. The huge, compound-curved backlight stands out as a case in point.

"We had an awful time getting that rear glass produced," says Chuck Jordan. "The problem was the flare and the shape. It's a convex backlight, but it flares out at the base. It was the S-shaped, curled glass that the suppliers couldn't produce the first time.

"We had to get this right," Jordan continues. "After all, the glass doesn't have any framing, and it fits into a very definite opening. At the end of the glass there's a beaver-tail—the sheetmetal panel. So you've got to have great accuracy in the shape of this glass."

Jerry Palmer adds, "If Chuck hadn't pushed the glass suppliers at the time, we probably wouldn't have that backlight today. Then, too, Cy Rappezi, who's the design engineer responsible for all of Design Staff's glass development—he and I made many, many trips to both LOF [Libbey-Owens-Ford] in Toledo and PPG [Pittsburgh Plate Glass] in Pittsburgh. We had a very close design relationship between us and the suppliers. Cy and I would go down just to talk design and get the aesthetics right. Working with the suppliers, making suggestions, helped them identify the problems."

At first, the glass suppliers doubted that an S-curved backlight could be mass produced at all, but after months of development, they finally formulated a process. Since both companies were involved in making the backlight possible, both LOF and PPG produce them for the Camaro and Firebird today.

Observes Dave Holls in retrospect, "The pivotal thing in this 1982 car was the new use of glass. We probably worked harder to get that than any other single item I can remember."

Attempts to keep the Camaro and Firebird distinctive and easily identifiable turned into another struggle, but of a different sort. Hughet's model had gone upstairs from Advanced One into Pontiac Two as a Firebird. It arrived in John Schinella's production studio with hidden headlights, a feature that Schinella wanted very much to keep for the '82 Bird.

Schinella had, in fact, campaigned hard for hidden headlamps before. He'd wanted them on the 1979-81 Firebird, especially on the Tenth Anniversary Trans Am. But Pontiac's cost accountants kept shooting him down. This time, though, John crossed his arms and wouldn't give in.

"When we got the 1982 car," Schinella explains, "the beancounters all said we weren't going to be able to get the hidden headlights. We went through a desperate search. But Al Mair supported the program and took it to the highest reaches of the corporation. Mair went up and told management, We will have aircraft technology and we'll have a small frontal mass for good aerodynamics. Eventually we got the hidden lights into production." Alex C. Mair was Pontiac's general manager at the time.

And Jerry Palmer went forward with fully exposed lamps for the 1982 Camaro. "We

1982 F RWD

Palmer and Schinella (Chevrolet and Pontiac production studio heads) vowed to keep their cars as different as possible despite shared roofs and glass.

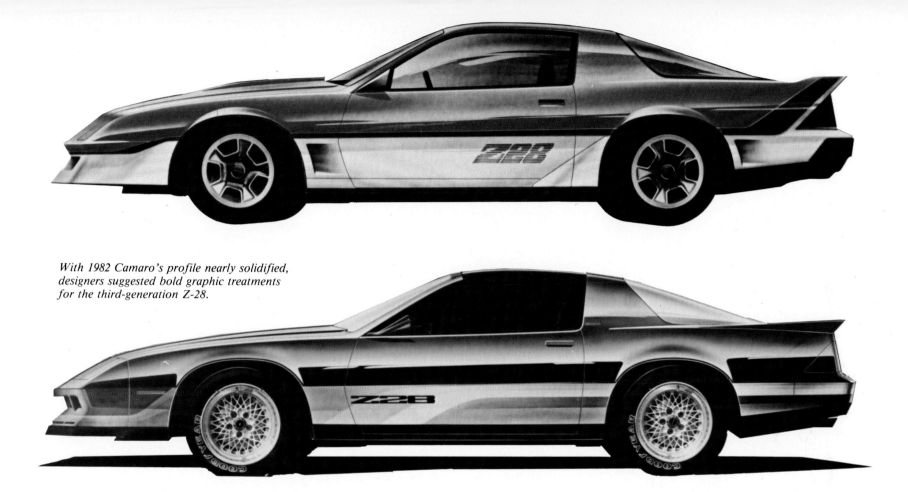

With 1982 Camaro's profile nearly solidified, designers suggested bold graphic treatments for the third-generation Z-28.

were innovative inasmuch as we came up with the hood that closes over the headlights. There's no bezel. In order to adjust these lamps, you have to pop the hood. In going this way, we saved another 1.5 inches in the car's overall height and, at the same time, achieved the wedge look.

"When you see the exposed-lamp Camaro," Palmer continues, "it has a sneaky look to it—sort of a mean look. So there isn't that startling a difference between the exposed-lamp Camaro and the hidden-lamp Bird."

After Schinella got the nod for flip-up headlights, both studios ironed out the technical details of sharing common "black metal." That's the term given black-painted structural items like radiator supports, bumper brackets, inner fenders, and similar hidden members identical in both cars.

Resolving the faces of these two automobiles proved a considerable triumph. Designers of first- and second-generation F-Cars had to contend with lookalike problems, too. But as it turns out, this third generation goes further than previous cars because the 1982 Camaro and Firebird share only uppers and doors.

That fact, though, didn't come easily. It took a lot of battles to make the two cars look different. Early directives said that the new Camaro and Firebird should share rear fenders and perhaps rear end caps as well.

Assistant executive designer Ed Taylor explains. "The '82 Camaro/Firebird program plan book called for the cars to have the same rear quarters. It specified more, not

fewer, interchangeable body surfaces than the previous generation. But as the program progressed, it became evident that we needed more design freedom to arrive at two distinctive, different-looking cars.

"The studios very much wanted separate rear quarters. This became an important point of design differentiation for both Jerry Palmer and John Schinella. So we made a plea to GM's top management people. Jim McDonald arrived [corporate vice president F. James McDonald] and quickly ascertained that unique quarter panels were indeed worth the extra few millions of dollars they would cost.

"This not only freed up the designs for total theme differences," continues Taylor, "but now the Firebird could have its original 'through' fender front to rear, and the Camaro could continue pursuing the 'monocoque rear quarter-to-upper' theme it had started with. It also meant the wheel-opening shapes could be different." This last became a very important area of differentiation.

Jerry Palmer adds, "The wheel cutouts make an interesting story. When Bill Porter and Roger Hughet started productionizing the Firebird downstairs, it had elliptical wheel openings. Our model upstairs had round openings. Then Irv [Rybicki] came in and said, 'You know, I think we've got these wheel openings backwards.' Irv felt that the Firebird should have the rounder openings, and we went to more rectangular cutouts.

"Irv also felt we were too soft with our wheel flares. We had a super-soft fillet around

Headlight covers, special graphics, revised tail lamps stand out among the European Camaro's suggested design attributes. For years, Camaros outsold

all other American cars in Germany, so GM decided to create a specific model— the GT-Z—for European market. GT-Z's hood includes raised central portion.

our wheel openings. The Firebird's was much more defined. Irv said, 'You know, on a car like this, the flares should be harder—more like applied flares.' So we modeled them that way, and Jeez they looked good! They gave the car a little more tautness; more of an accent. It was the right thing to do, because both cars now have a nice quality about them, with a balance of softness and severity.''

And Ed Taylor concludes, ''Different rear quarters meant not only that the wheel openings could be unique to each car, but the bonus in all this was a saving to Chevrolet, because the Camaro no longer had the penalty of needing rear-quarter end caps. End caps tend to be expensive, and the quality of the caps and the way they're mounted can be hard to control.''

The new Camaro's ''face'' or front theme also went through a number of changes. ''We started out with a louvered grille theme,'' recalls Jerry Palmer, ''very similar to the 1981 Z-28. But we just weren't happy with that. Management wanted an upper and lower grille, but that didn't work out because the front end looked too small.

''So we finally got into this integrated airdam with the smooth forehead above the bumper peak. We felt, though, that it needed something for good down-the-road identity, so we added the three ports on the base Sport Coupe and the Berlinetta, with the Cibie driving lamps as parking lights.

''That pretty much locked in the Sport Coupe and Berlinetta, but then we had to do

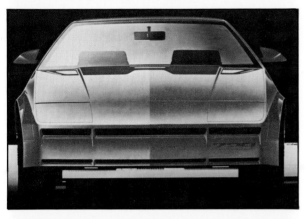

To distinguish it from the Firebird, Camaro needed exposed quad headlamps. Palmer recognized and welcomed this. Upper and lower grilles made face look too narrow, so mouth-like air intake evolved, with smooth forehead for Z-28 and tri-slots for Berlinetta and Sport Coupe. Soft fascia allowed hidden bumper and integrated airdam, with Z eventually getting parking lamps tucked into pseudo brake air inlets plus cold-air NACA ducts with TBI hood flappers.

Compound-curved rear glass was particularly hard to form, and at one point both glass suppliers deemed it impossible. Raised spoiler, fender air outlets were tried and rejected.

Camaro's familiar slash tail lights were never in doubt, give new generation recognizability and continuity with the past.

One thought combined modified whale tail, horizontal lenses with Z-28 script.

As they approached 1982 Camaro's final shape and detailing by the summer of '78, Palmer's design group firmly resolved to shun unnecessary frills and ornamentation. Finished car's only brightwork is in its wheels.

the Z-28 front. Irv and Ed Taylor felt that the Z-28 should work without any slots—that it should have a smooth forehead. So we ended up using black-lens parking and directional lamps that look like brake air intakes in the *off* position. With the centered theme and the slots down below—plus the ground-effects look of the Z-28 airdam and the 15-inch Ferrari-looking wheels (we stole them right off the Ferrari)—the car forms a unique, fresh-looking design. The Z front end is about two inches longer than the other models, and the ground-effects airdam is right under the chin, not tucked back like the Berlinetta and the base car."

About the rear, Palmer comments, "The rear became an evolution of the second-generation Camaro's. We felt the Camaro's rear graphics are as strong as any in the business. I was pretty much responsible for the wrap-around diagonal slash back for the

1974 Camaro, under Hank Haga. That's become our trademark. I see a lot of cars using it now, but the '82 Camaro's makes our car very identifiable."

Even when a design goes smoothly, which the 1982 F-Car program didn't, one battle looms constantly in the background. That's the fight against time. There's never enough and, as you know, Design Staff had been handed a very tight deadline. Full-sized clays of the '82 Camaro and Firebird had to be finished by Dec. 11, 1978 for management review.

The production studios received and set about refining Hughet's theme in Feb. 1978. That left only 10 months to prepare a practical, full-scale clay model. So Jerry Palmer and John Schinella—the Camaro and Firebird production studio heads—began using every tool and trick in their arsenal.

One of Design Staff's front-line weapons against time turns out to be the computer. Computers played a tremendous role in developing the third-generation Camaro's surfaces, so it's appropriate here to explore the function of computers in evolving the F-Car's designs. Computers are turning out to be just as indispensable to stylists as to engineers, and they promise to do even more in the future.

Jerry Palmer points out that computers were used more extensively in the F-Car's design development than in any other program ever attempted at General Motors. "It was the first car started here where all the *front loading* was computer programmed," says Palmer. "When we designed this car, every move was kept up to date in the computer."

What Palmer means by "front loading" is that all the F-Car's engineering data had been put into the computer beforehand—even before the studios began to work on paper. Dimensions like wheelbase, length, height, width; specifications telling the various engine positions and shapes; cowl, windshield, door-pillar, and fuel-tank placement; axle and suspension locations; wheel-house sizes; firewall and plenum positionings; seat, floor, and roof limits—all these specs and locations plus dozens more were already stored and accessible inside the computer.

So when a designer would draw, for example, a hoodline, he then handed that silhouette to a studio technician, who put the line into the computer. If there weren't, say, enough hood clearance for the Z-28's twin throttle-body injectors, the computer would flash a light and show outlines of the TBI sticking up through the hood surface.

There's no doubt in my mind that GM leads the industry in computer-aided auto design. It's not yet effective for an aesthetic designer to sit at a computer console and "draw" with a light probe. So far, it's still more practical to design with paper and pencil. Once that's done, though, the technical stylist can translate the sketch or mechanical drawing from paper to screen. And once the sketch is inside the computer, the designer can see and check it not only in two dimensions but more often in three.

In other words, he can "walk around" the car almost as if it were in clay. The drawing can be turned to any angle on the screen. Better than that, the designer can have the technician input such specific items as doors, hinges, hood, decklid, trunk, and seats. That way he can check whether doors bind against fenders or drag against curbs; whether windows roll all the way up and down; whether rear passengers get too much sunlight through a glass hatch, and so on. He can even "load" a trunk with suitcases and boxes of different sizes—do this right on the screen—and can change the trunk shape to accommodate more cargo by, say, raising the decklid line or shifting the spare tire around. This can all happen on a computer screen long before the car goes into metal.

So you can see that the computer becomes a marvelous tool even in this relatively simple function. Beyond that, it allows different studios to keep track of each other's work without making and pointing out actual physical changes on a clay model. Jerry Palmer might decide to change the shape of a headlight receptacle on the '82 Camaro. This could move the F-Car's black metal, say, an inch rearward, which in turn might affect the operation of John Schinella's hidden headlights. With the appropriate data in the computer, a compromise could be worked out to make both studio chiefs happy. And, in fact, just such computerized give and take did happen several times. Compromises could be reached right on the computer screen.

But even *those* examples show the computer in its simplest aspect. One of the most impressive and basic add-ons to the computer is what's called a *digital coordinate recorder* (DCR or "digitizer"). This takes the form of a scanner that can "see" or "read" a clay model and can translate or store the clay's three dimensions on a long Mylar or punched paper tape.

The digitizer comes in several forms, but imagine the basic machine as a light probe on the end of a metal rod. The rod attaches to a stand that lets the light probe move in or out, up or down in a predetermined pattern. The light probe and its stand are wheeled over to a clay model—and this can be either a scale model or full-sized; either a half model against a mirror or one that's freestanding—and the tech stylist flicks on a

switch. The probe begins to move but never touches the clay. It keeps itself an inch or so away from the clay's surface.

As it moves—first up the full side of the model, then rearward a tiny bit, then down to the floor, rearward again, up, etc., its movements are being recorded or digitized as three sets of numbers. The numbers represent the X, Y, and Z coordinates on a 3-dimensional graph.

After the digitizer finishes scanning the entire model or any chosen part of it, several different things can be done with the resulting tape. It can be fed into a clay-milling machine, for example, which duplicates the original model in clay somewhere else. And the duplicate needn't be the same size. The clay-milling machine can be programmed to turn out a full-sized clay from a tiny scale model, or vice-versa.

Nor need the duplicate clay be in the same room or even the same country. GM can and does originate clay models at Opel in Germany, then digitizes them and sends the computer information via phone or satellite to Warren, Mich., where, say, a clay-milling machine unscrambles the encoded numbers and produces an identical clay model—a duplicate of the original that's located 4400 miles distant.

I must mention as an aside that the clay-milling machine doesn't immediately produce a perfect replica of the original. It cuts grooves in shapeless clay, which then must be hand finished by a human modeler. The amount of work the modeler has to do, though, depends on how far apart the milled grooves lie from one another. They can be programmed to be close together or several inches apart.

Now that's not all that digitizing can do. The same taped information that drives the clay-milling machine can also drive numerically controlled grinders, cutters, or lathes that can form the shape of the original clay in wood or metal. You can zero in on any specific part of the clay, too—say a headlamp housing of the 1982 Camaro—and get that one piece carved out of metal or plastic. So in theory if not in practice, a designer could order up a metal part of a car that didn't yet exist and could "prove it out" on his clay model—see if the shape could be formed, how reflections would look, whether screw heads or fasteners would detract, etc.

Of course, 2-dimensional scale drawings or 3-dimensional video-terminal display drawings can also be generated from digitized information. Body engineers see the day when sheetmetal releases can be made directly from digitized information, some garnered straight from clay models. GM even predicts that holograms will spring from digitized data, and holograms might either supplement or replace clay models and/or fiberglass mockups.

At any rate, the computer, the digitizer, and clay-milling machines were used more extensively in developing the final surfaces of the third-generation Camaro than for any car done previously.

Another tool used to great advantage throughout the F-Car program was the wind-tunnel. General Motors now has its own tunnel—manned by GM Engineering's aerodynamics laboratory—on the Technical Center premises behind the Design Staff building. This windtunnel, though, wasn't finished until 1980, so most of the aerodynamic tuning of full-sized Camaro clay models went on in the Lockheed-Marietta tunnel near Atlanta, Ga.

The procedure is as follows, and I'll let Charles (Chuck) Torner, executive engineer with Design Staff's advanced engineering department, explain. Torner directs Design Staff's aero activity.

"Typically," he says, "we test third- or quarter-scale models first, because that way it's easier and quicker to make major changes than with a full-scale clay. When we put the scale model into the tunnel, it's fully detailed underneath—has the outlines of the suspension system, engine oil pan, transmission, gas tank, differential housing, and so forth. We simulate airflow through the radiator, and we install outside mirrors.

"We like to get in while the car is still in the advanced studio," continues Torner. "If the advanced model shows a high drag coefficient [Cd], we know we've got to look for another theme. The simplest way to check airflow for a scale model is to put ink

Windtunnel testing—first of scale models and then of full-sized clays—went on continuously throughout the F-Car program. To check airflow patterns, *technicians attached yarn (left) and used ink droplets (right). Models have fully detailed undersides. The final Camaro clay tested out at a Cd of 0.37.*

droplets on the clay or attach yarn tufts. That way we can see the airflow pattern and make improvements."

The clay car rests on a spring-supported platform inside the windtunnel, and the platform moves to register not only drag but also front- and rear-end lift and downforces. Scale F-Car models were tested in GM's Harrison windtunnel at the Technical Center. Full-scale clays now go into General Motors' new big tunnel, which can generate wind velocities up to 124 mph. High-speed winds, though, are used for work with reduced-scale models. Full-scale testing is usually done at about 50 mph.

"GM was the first U.S. automaker," states Torner, "to do windtunnel work with complete, full-sized clay models. Again, the model has a special armature under it to replicate the full underbody of a real car, including engine compartment and running gear. For the 1982 F-Car, we packed up the clay here and sent it down to Lockheed-Marietta. This was the only U.S. facility available until we built our own tunnel. It was a Firebird clay, I remember, and John Schinella went down with it.

"I remember that John [Schinella] nearly got killed on that Firebird test. They were unloading the model off the truck, and the left-side ramp broke loose. John was standing right there by the ramp. If there hadn't been jacks under the ramp, the model would have fallen right on top of John, and it probably would have killed him. Luckily the jacks held, but he had a close shave."

Torner pauses at this point and then goes on. "Aerodynamics is part of the design discipline. We literally never run a test without a designer there. We can't dictate design or design direction. The designer's responsible for what the car looks like. We can only suggest and recommend.

"Our philosophy is to include the designer in all reduced and full-scale testing work. He's right there inside the tunnel, working with the rest of the guys."

The F-Car aero team included Robert Chamberlin, Frank Meinert, and L. Nealy, lead engineers from Design Staff, GM Engineering, and Chevrolet Engineering respectively, plus a group of sculptors and technicians.

"Reducing aerodynamic drag," adds Torner, "is an effective way to improve fuel economy. If we can improve a model with, say, a Cd of 0.50 to 0.40, the resulting car—if it got 30 mpg before—will now get approximately 31.8 mpg. All we've done is bend a little sheetmetal. We've come to the point where it's very hard to remove more weight from any given car, but the field of aerodynamics is still wide open."

For tunnel testing, GM now uses a movable fixture that simulates the front airdam of a car. This fixture can be positioned beneath the front bumper pan of a model and can be shifted forward or rearward to improve airflow. The airdam's vee angle can also be adjusted.

Add-on rear spoilers of different types and shapes can be fixed to the deck of a model. Fender skirts are sometimes found to improve a car's Cd, and some were tried on early Firebird scale models, as were flush-fitting wheelcovers.

"GM also has a system," adds Chuck Torner, "to measure the wind-rush noise over the side glass of a vehicle. We work with proving-grounds engineers to install an anechoic [non-echo, sound-absorbing] chamber with microphones inside specially prepared full-scale clay models. We can then change such aspects as the A-pillar shape or angle, the side glass, windshield, etc., to tune these items for the quietest sound. It's another dimension of what we're able to do in the tunnel."

The 1982 Camaro had an aerodynamic target of Cd 0.36. As it turns out, the full-sized clay model actually beat that. It registered Cd 0.35. The finished car tests out at Cd 0.37, which is one of the lowest drag coefficients ever measured by General Motors for a production automobile.

One reason for this low Cd is the very "fast" or laid-back windshield angle. The Camaro's windshield has a 62-degree slope—the most acute angle of any GM windshield ever produced. In fact, GM engineering guidelines specify that no windshield should have an angle steeper than 60 degrees. F-Car designers felt the 62-degree glass was needed for aesthetic reasons, but that alone wouldn't have prompted GM to go against its own guidelines. What finally caused the 62-degree windshield to pass was the fact that Chevrolet vehicles engineer Tom Zimmer convinced management that the fast windshield contributed to the '82 Camaro's low Cd and thus helped improve its fuel economy.

Notes Jerry Palmer, "We got the 62-degree windshield because the people in Engineering, particularly Tom Zimmer and Don Urban, stood behind us and fought with us to keep it. They mocked up a 1978 Camaro with a 62.5-degree windshield. Fisher Body was totally against it, as were some people at Pontiac. So they had a ride-and-drive at the proving ground with this '78 F-Car with the 62.5-degree glass, and Zimmer liked it better than the regular '78. There really wasn't any argument."

Stresses Zimmer: "Those aero numbers on the '82 Camaro are as low as the corporation has ever measured. That isn't to say they're the lowest in the world, but we haven't

On a chilly Dec. 12, 1978, GM management warmly approved Design Staff's fiberglass Z-28. *Except for minor revisions, production version looks like this.*

measured any that are lower. And the low aero numbers have resulted in a good break for us on fuel economy.''

The 1982 Camaro emerged from Chevy Three on schedule in Dec. 1978 and received enthusiastic approval from everyone up and down the line. GM's top managers smiled a lot that day, and they happily shook hands with the man principally responsible for the car's shape and detailing.

Jerry P. Palmer grew up in Detroit, the son of a successful Pontiac salesman. ''My dad was a car nut,'' says Palmer, ''and by age three, I was one myself.'' He sketched cars throughout high school and, in 1961, enrolled in Detroit's Society for Arts and Crafts—now renamed the Center for Creative Studies. Among his instructors were veteran designer Homer LaGassey and Tucker/Ford stylist Alex Tremulis.

At the same time he was going to art school, Palmer also held jobs with Gus Pernack's Applied Industries and Creative Industries. At Applied Industries, a Detroit tool-and-die shop, Jerry machined prototype parts for Ford, Chrysler, and GM. ''My best education,'' he says. And at Creative Industries, a small design firm, he worked on the futuristic U.S. Steel Innovari, among other cars.

After his junior year at Arts and Crafts, Palmer joined a GM summer design program, which led to his being hired in 1966 into a special GM design development studio. Jerry became the first graduate of the Center for Creative Studies ever to be granted a permanent position with GM Design Staff.

Palmer was later transferred to Advanced Four, where he worked on the boattail Riviera. In 1967, he joined Henry (Hank) Haga, who was just finishing up the 1970½ Camaro in Chevy Two. Palmer became involved in the Camaro kammback wagon and in detailing the second-generation Z-28. He worked principally, though, on the Vega.

Eventually Palmer became Haga's assistant, and about that time Chevy Three became a satellite of the Chevy Two studio, with Haga taking on the Camaro, Corvette, Vega, and Monza. Hank and Jerry, under the direction of William L. Mitchell, did the Aero Vette—the Corvette with the rotary engine.

When Hank Haga was assigned to head Opel design in Germany in June 1974, Palmer became head of Chevy Three. Thus Jerry has been responsible for all second-generation Camaro styling updates from the 1975 model on.

Eighteen months after Roger Hughet's model was chosen as the 1982 F-Car's inspiration and theme, Hughet himself went up from Advanced One to Chevy Three and became Palmer's assistant. So these two designers headed the team that did the actual hands on development of the 1982 Camaro's exterior.

Final touches had to be added even after the management show of mid-Dec. 1978. Fiberglass mockups followed in Feb. 1979, and steel prototypes, with body skins reflecting the final design, were assembled in Mar. 1980.

Design director Chuck Jordan comments: ''I was out at the GM Proving Grounds in Milford, Mich., and this was the first time I'd seen the Camaro outdoors, running. We took the present Camaro [1981] and the 1982 Camaro, both Z's, and got out in front of them, watching them come up over a hill and run together. This was on a truck test loop—a two-lane road.

''Then we followed behind them for a while, and finally we got way out ahead and watched them go by at speed. We kept doing that. Wow, what an experience! That new, sleek car—it's got its head down, looks mean as anything coming over those rises. I was particularly struck with the front views. Now the 1981 car—it's not bad-looking, but it looks fat when you see the two cars together. The contrast makes you realize the shock value that this new car has. It's simple, pure, and lean compared with the older car. To get them together on the street shows up the impact of this new car. I don't know a guy who isn't enthused about it.''

In Dec. 1980, on a big corporate ride-and-drive near Phoenix, Ariz., motorists in other cars were so surprised and curious about the 1982 Camaro prototypes that flashed by that some actually caused accidents.

''In back of the hotel, early in the morning,'' continues Jordan, ''we took out four prototypes—two Camaros and two Firebirds—plus some other cars for comparison, and the 1982 F-Cars did cause accidents. Some guy in a 1981 Camaro...I was back behind the prototypes, near the end of the line, and we were coming up to a stop. This fellow in the Camaro saw one of the '82 Camaros go by. He knew it was a Camaro, and he got so excited that he went *bang*, right into the back of another car that had stopped. Here was this poor guy by the time I got there, sitting there, the glass all broken out of one headlight, the grille smashed, and I felt really sorry for him. On the other hand, I thought, Well, that's the mark of a successful design if you can get a guy to smash his car just craning to look at the new one. That's a real testimonial.'' □

Chapter Two

Creating an Entirely New Interior

Advanced Studio's Ideas Win Out

GEORGE R. ANGERSBACH, you'll remember, was the man who'd come up with the double-bent instrument panel for the 1970½-78 Camaro. George had originally sketched this design on a napkin one day at lunch.

And William D. (Bill) Scott later conceived the 1979-81 Camaro instrument panel (i.p.)—the one and only revision to the second generation's dashboard layout. Scott had been Chevrolet's chief interior designer since Dec. 1974.

As in second generation, Camaro interior designers vowed to keep gauges highly visible and controls within easy reach. Early proposal centered graphic display above console.

Angersbach and Scott teamed again to create the third generation Camaro's interior, and they worked under the supervision of GM's executive interior designer, George E. Moon. Angersbach, in fact, was and remains Moon's assistant. As such, he heads Design Staff's Interior Concepts studio, an area that amounts basically to Interior's version of an advanced studio.

Bill Scott remained chief designer of Chevrolet's interior production studio throughout the time of the '82 Camaro's development. He's now, however, Pontiac's chief interior designer.

Both Scott's production studio and Angersbach's concepts studio had been working independently on a third-generation Camaro interior. Scott remembers that, "...we'd

both been struggling for almost 18 months before we got the go-ahead to do the real thing. We'd done some work toward the 1980 program, but that got scrapped while the engineering guys were sorting out front drive versus rear drive.

"So when we got going again for 1982, we picked up some of those older themes, and once in a while we have competitive contests among the various studios. Contests stimulate people to get things off dead center. Well, we in Chevrolet Interiors lost out to George's concepts studio—we lost the contest to Concepts because their initial panel got the best reviews. We at Chevrolet had our noses out of joint for a few weeks, but we got over it."

In explaining the goals of that contest, GM Design vice president Irv Rybicki has this to say: "As in the second generation, we wanted a very driver-oriented interior. The individual who buys a Camaro is very sensitive to steering and shifter position, wants all the controls at his fingertips, wants sports-car seating, and has to have the instruments where he can watch them at all times.

"We did spend a lot of time on paper and in the seating buck just getting everything properly located. You can read every dial either through the steering wheel or outside the wheel.

"A lot of time went into packaging the interior compartment," stresses Mr. Rybicki. "Our bogie was to equal all the dimensions we'd had inside the previous Camaro, but we did better than that in some instances. For example, if you get into the back seat, you'll find there's a lot more space in this smaller, narrower, shorter car than you had in the '81 Camaro. We were able to provide almost two inches more shoulder room plus more knee room in our new rear compartment, along with having a hatch and the utility that goes with that."

Angersbach's original concept instrument panel, mocked up in Aug. 1978, pretty much set the direction for the finished product. The main 2-dial gauge cluster flanked by fingertip pods behind the steering rim—those items never changed. Nor did the long, recessed area to the right.

Says George Angersbach: "The Chevrolet interior production studio had been working on the 1982 F-Car instrument panel for some time before we got the concept studio involved. Although I was in charge of that area, the concept studios reported directly to John Shettler. Marv Fisher, as assistant chief designer, and Julian Carter, designer, were the major contributors to the initial design from which the '82 Camaro and Firebird instrument panels evolved."

"We were still toying at that time with an electronic readout above the console," notes Bill Scott. "But finally we found there wouldn't be space for one even if we could afford it, which was doubtful. As for space, by the time we got the ECM boxes packaged behind the i.p., there simply wasn't enough space even for a glovebox. We put the glovebox in the tunnel console. [ECM stands for *electronic control module*, the microprocessor that controls the TBI.]

"Along with the graphic readout, we'd proposed a series of pushbuttons. We felt these would be neat. You have the important controls at your fingertips near the steering wheel, but then your other switches for a proposed sunroof, power windows, rear

Designers knew that to prevent reflections or "veiling glare" in 62-degree windshield, gauges had to tuck beneath a matte-black deck in all Camaros.

Low horizontal spokes on Z-28 wheel (early version shown) allow clear view of gauges. Designers use heavy creased paper to show mockup panel contours.

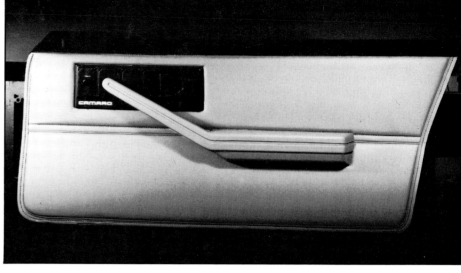

Since all Camaros now come with standard console, designers knew they could integrate it with main panel; also use it for radio, heater, and other controls.

Door panels came in for careful study, particularly integration of escutcheon with pull release handle, mirror joystick, and electric or manual door locks.

defroster, road lamps, etc., were in a punchboard just beneath the central air-conditioner outlets. That, too, went away as the program evolved,''

The '82 Camaro's 62-degree windshield became a concern to Angersbach and Scott for exactly the reasons the GM engineering guidebook says it's too steep. "We had the most severely raked windshield to deal with of any production GM car to date," mentions George Angersbach. "We in interiors have to be careful of what we call *veiling glare*. This means you have to keep all lit surfaces from reflecting in the glass, and to do that we had to put a large hood on the panel. The hood, though, creates another type of daytime veiling glare, which reflects the hood itself back up into the windshield.''

Bill Scott elaborates: "What we did was to create this aircraft-carrier-like hood that extends back into the car. We then pushed the i.p. forward underneath that, which led to the freestanding cluster unit. In other words, you throw this big wing across the top and hang the pod beneath it, and that gives the passenger plenty of room on his side to cross his legs or whatever.

"Then we went to a very flat, black, light-absorbing finish to keep the veiling glare down out of the glass. The black theme extends onto the door, garnish moldings, and A-pillars. We said, Okay, that black finish should be there on every car. The pad and cluster for every model of 1982 Camaro are black, but at first we wanted to color-key the backset panel and knee pad. Unfortunately that would have involved masking and painting, and the money boys said no. There've been some reviews by some high company officials who feel black is too harsh, especially in the Berlinetta, but the division has stood firm with black so far.''

Bill Scott continues: "We wanted to get the instruments big, with bold dials—clean and clear. One problem, though, involved this government requirement that we now include kilometers on the speedometer scale along with miles per hour. Every time I wanted to put the second row of numbers around the speedometer, it seemed cluttered.

"So one of the guys in the studio, Jon Albert, drew a sketch where he had a double-ended pointer. You read the metric kilometer scale on one side and the English mph scale on the other. Everyone thought that was a super idea. We mocked it up, and it was enthusiastically accepted.

"Every once in a while someone in the studio does something that everybody likes, and it goes right through. This dual pointer was one of the best examples. It's a new,

good, interesting idea, and it's fun to look at. Best of all, it didn't cost anything. And Jon Albert should get the credit.''

Chevrolet had made the tunnel console standard equipment in all Camaros for 1981, even in the base Sport Coupe. This meant that a console would again become standard for '82 and could be built in not as an afterthought or a sometimes accessory but as an integral part of every car.

Non-integral consoles, as in first- and second-generation Camaros, had to have certain tolerances or actual gaps between the instrument panel and the console itself. That's so the console wouldn't squeak or rub against the lower edge of the i.p. These gaps have always been distasteful to designers. So with the 1982 Camaro came an opportunity to integrate the console into the i.p., giving both units a one-piece look, without gaps or the appearance of an add-on.

"Chuck Jordan and Jerry Palmer and I took a little trip to the Grumman aircraft plant one day to look at the F-14's," reminisces Bill Scott. "Those F-14's have gauges everywhere—on the ceiling, on side panels, on horizontal surfaces. So we took the console's horizontal surface as a novel location for the rally clock, and I feel it adds to the overall performance appearance of the Camaro.

"Meanwhile, we'll be offering the Delco 2000-series radio in this car. The tape-playing versions of this radio include a digital clock, so instead of giving the customer two clocks in the Berlinetta and Z-28, we delete the console clock. It's possible, of course, to special-order both clocks, and some people undoubtedly will for the two different functions.''

Let's talk now about the 1982 Camaro's front bucket seats, particularly the new Conteur adjustable sculptured seat. The Conteur seat was another of those items that needed championing. It didn't just happen.

Fisher Body Div., which builds seats for all GM car divisions, likes to deal in high-volume seats that can be built up from compact, easy-to-store and -assemble elements. The Conteur seat isn't that type.

"We're very pleased to have gotten that optional Conteur seat," comments Chevrolet vehicles engineer Tom Zimmer, "and we're very proud of it, because it's unique to the 1982 Camaro. For the first time, we're going to offer the sort of seat we've been after for years, namely a fully adjustable driver's seat.

"It has all the adjustments—thigh support, lateral bolster adjustment on the cushion and seatback, lumbar adjustment, adjustable headrests, seatback angle, and you can get

Double pointer for speedometer was an innovation conceived by interior designer Jon Albert. One scale shows speed in mph, the other in kilometers.

Console rally clock had its inspiration from Grumman F-14. Vent at front of console pushes warm or cool air between and under seats to rear riders.

the seat in any 1982 Z-28, with or without the up-level interior. Now the way we're offering it—you get it on the driver's side only. The passenger's seat doesn't have the full Conteur range of adjustments. The right front bucket is the standard seat trimmed to match the Conteur."

Bill Scott adds, "It's hard for us to sell a new idea to Fisher Body if it's not high volume. And I'd say that, although Design Staff has always been pressing for better seating in this car, we couldn't achieve that alone. I have to give great credit to Tom Zimmer for pushing the Conteur seat through to production. Fisher Body didn't want to make it, so Tom and I went to Lear-Siegler and talked to them about helping us out on this third-generation's seating. We wanted an articulated seat—adjustable—the sort you see from Recaro and Scheel and others like that. We particularly wanted it for the Z-28; wanted a super performance seat for that car.

"We began working the thing out with Lear-Siegler, and Lear-Siegler is now building the frame for Fisher Body. Fisher is trimming it in a regular trim plant. What happens—these seats are delivered to the assembly plant trimmed. This means they take up a lot of plant storage space. You've got the frame and the buns and the seat, whereas the normal procedure for assembly is that the frame comes in in one package. The buns come in another, and they're easily stacked, soft pieces. The trim covers normally come in already sewn together, flat and in a stack. When the seat needs to go together, a worker takes the frame, puts on the bun, takes a trim cover and skins it down over the seat.

"But you can't do that with a fully trimmed seat like the Centeur," Scott continues. "They come in and each one takes up its own individual space. You can't stack them as efficiently. So that led Fisher to put a capacity limit on the Conteur seat. We at Chevrolet, though, anticipated more demand for the Conteur than Fisher is willing to give us space, and this led us to stop and ask, Should we offer two such seats in one car or one seat in each of two cars?"

Chevrolet broke precedent with the '82 Z-28 by offering the Conteur on the driver's side only. In looks, shape, and function, it doesn't quite match the passenger's seat, even though both are trimmed identically. Yet the average passerby probably wouldn't notice that the two seats are different.

"Tom Zimmer felt that to make this car really driver-oriented," Scott adds, "we should make the Conteur optional on the driver's side only. And by doing that, we can install it in twice as many cars.''

While the Conteur seat takes the spotlight, "...I want to talk about the base seat, too, because it's nothing to be taken lightly," Bill Scott points out. "It's the standard J-Car seat, and the development work that went into that J-Car seat is considerable.

"The J seat is shared in three cars. It's part of the 1982 T-Car custom interior, the J-Car's standard interior, and now the F-Car's standard interior, all in the same fabrics. It's trimmed either in vinyl or cloth. The cloth we use is called Millport, and it's a very sporty, tweedy fabric. When we decided to make the Conteur seat an option, it worked out well because we took the Millport and used it on the seating surface insert, so it looks good and feels good. The base F-Car buckets include a good measure of lumbar support plus the recliner. Recliners are standard."

For 1983, the passenger's seat will be revised to have a separate headrest. It'll still be basically the J-Car seat, but it'll look more like the Conteur.

Bill Scott's designers strongly recommended splitting the rear seatback for the 1982 Camaro. Chevrolet's bookkeepers said no; in fact, they initially insisted that the rear seatback should be fixed! Bill Scott rolled his eyes and, by his own account, moaned, "...I told them, Holy cripes, if you want the magazine writers to crucify us, let's go ahead and provide a fixed rear seatback! I said right from the start that the seatback should be split and each side fold separately. Design Staff certainly wanted that. I'm sure Engineering did, too. What if three people want to go skiing? Or you travel with a dog? Or carry groceries and a couple of kids? But after we'd fought with the accountants about the split rear seatback, they finally at least gave us one that folds."

The interior designers knew they had the outside mirror controls coming into the door; also the pushbuttons for the electric and manual door locks plus buckle-type interior door handles, so their thoughts ran toward integrating all these elements in one pod. "That way we could clean up the clutter on the door," comments Scott. "Sometimes we look at a door and think it must have been designed with a shotgun."

As it stands, everything fits neatly into what's almost a horizontal console. It looks high tech and businesslike, with functional Torx-head screws complementing those on the i.p. Each element of the door pod is easy to see and reach.

Susanne Gatchell, Ph.D., is the person responsible for the F-Car's human accommodations at Fisher Body, which means trying to make everything touched or handled by a driver or passenger comfortable and convenient—"friendly," as she calls it. On the

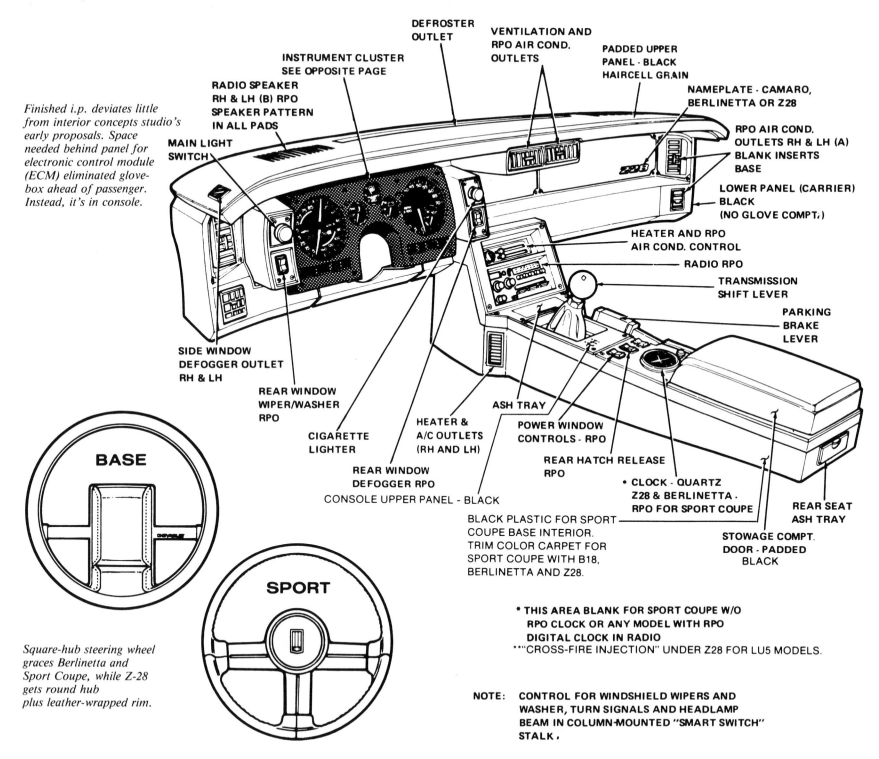

DEFROSTER OUTLET

VENTILATION AND RPO AIR COND. OUTLETS

PADDED UPPER PANEL - BLACK HAIRCELL GRAIN

INSTRUMENT CLUSTER SEE OPPOSITE PAGE

NAMEPLATE - CAMARO, BERLINETTA OR Z28

RADIO SPEAKER RH & LH (B) RPO SPEAKER PATTERN IN ALL PADS

Finished i.p. deviates little from interior concepts studio's early proposals. Space needed behind panel for electronic control module (ECM) eliminated glove-box ahead of passenger. Instead, it's in console.

MAIN LIGHT SWITCH

RPO AIR COND. OUTLETS RH & LH (A) BLANK INSERTS BASE

LOWER PANEL (CARRIER) BLACK (NO GLOVE COMPT.)

HEATER AND RPO AIR COND. CONTROL

RADIO RPO

TRANSMISSION SHIFT LEVER

PARKING BRAKE LEVER

SIDE WINDOW DEFOGGER OUTLET RH & LH

REAR WINDOW WIPER/WASHER RPO

CIGARETTE LIGHTER

HEATER & A/C OUTLETS (RH AND LH)

ASH TRAY

POWER WINDOW CONTROLS - RPO

REAR HATCH RELEASE RPO

REAR SEAT ASH TRAY

REAR WINDOW DEFOGGER RPO

CONSOLE UPPER PANEL - BLACK

• CLOCK - QUARTZ Z28 & BERLINETTA . RPO FOR SPORT COUPE

STOWAGE COMPT. DOOR - PADDED BLACK

BLACK PLASTIC FOR SPORT COUPE BASE INTERIOR. TRIM COLOR CARPET FOR SPORT COUPE WITH B18, BERLINETTA AND Z28.

BASE

SPORT

Square-hub steering wheel graces Berlinetta and Sport Coupe, while Z-28 gets round hub plus leather-wrapped rim.

* THIS AREA BLANK FOR SPORT COUPE W/O RPO CLOCK OR ANY MODEL WITH RPO DIGITAL CLOCK IN RADIO
**"CROSS-FIRE INJECTION" UNDER Z28 FOR LU5 MODELS.

NOTE: CONTROL FOR WINDSHIELD WIPERS AND WASHER, TURN SIGNALS AND HEADLAMP BEAM IN COLUMN-MOUNTED "SMART SWITCH" STALK.

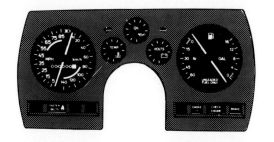

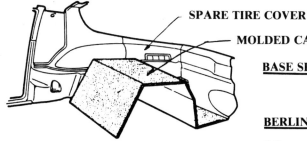

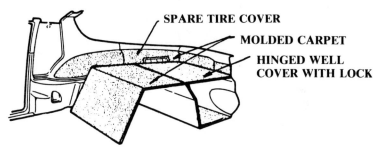

SPARE TIRE COVER

MOLDED CARPET

BASE SPORT COUPE & Z-28

BERLINETTA OR RPO B48

SPARE TIRE COVER

MOLDED CARPET

HINGED WELL COVER WITH LOCK

Base gauge cluster (top) uses warning lights, while Z-28 and Berlinetta have full working gauges. Berlinetta also comes with plusher cargo deck, well cover, and locking rear side compartment.

topic of the Camaro's new door-release system, Sue states, "We ran clinics on the car, and what we wanted to be sure of was that the inside door handles had adequate clearance, that the edges had adequate radii, and that the escutcheon and locking mechanism are friendly.

"The power door locks, as you've probably noticed, are the touch-sensitive type. Like a calculator. There were some complaints about these initially. People came back saying the switches were in the wrong locations and didn't feel good. Their effort was too high. So now we've got it down to a nice, low effort, and they're very comfortable to use.

"We also worked on the snorkle or pull handle on the armrest. There wasn't adequate clearance to get your hand behind it initially. We improved that; increased it

slightly. We looked at just about everything on this car—exterior door handles, door and hatch closing efforts, key access. We worked on the Conteur seat, too, to make sure its actions were good. We ended up redesigning some of the knobs and controls on that seat."

Continuing with the Conteur seat, Sue Gatchell elaborates that, "...I was even concerned about people who are fairly wide, because the Conteur is a narrower seat than normal. Our image of sports-car drivers is tall, thin, and lean. Yet we got some pretty broad-beamed people in our clinics. They liked the Conteur. It fit them. We didn't make any direct comparisons with so-called competition seats, but the Conteur isn't overly tight, it's not overly firm, and I frankly don't feel Americans are ready for those really hard, tight, hip-grabbing seats anyhow. The Conteurs are just right." □

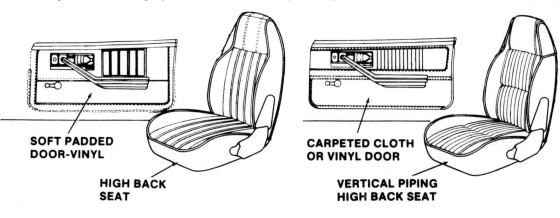

SOFT PADDED DOOR-VINYL

HIGH BACK SEAT

CARPETED CLOTH OR VINYL DOOR

VERTICAL PIPING HIGH BACK SEAT

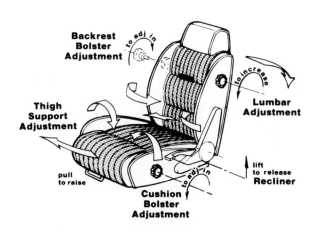

Backrest Bolster Adjustment

to adj in

to increase

Lumbar Adjustment

Thigh Support Adjustment

pull to raise

to adj in

lift to release Recliner

Cushion Bolster Adjustment

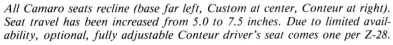

All Camaro seats recline (base far left, Custom at center, Conteur at right). Seat travel has been increased from 5.0 to 7.5 inches. Due to limited availability, optional, fully adjustable Conteur driver's seat comes one per Z-28.

Chapter Three

Engineering Ponderables–Fwd or Rwd?

Emphasis on Handling and Structure

Beginning in April 1979, engineers cobbled 12 Buick Skylark coupes to serve as Camaro pre-prototypes, converting them to rwd. Skylark bodies came close to eventual Camaro in size and rocker structure; could also accept the contemplated large rear backlight.

Even before work began on pre-prototypes, Camaro component cars or "mules" evolved by grafting Malibu front frames and suspension onto Monza

body sections. Engineers used these F-Car 1978 mules to explore suspension systems, engine placement, weight distribution, and to do early handling tests.

THIS TIME AROUND, Chevrolet engineers took a different approach to the Camaro. They decided to start with the Z-28 first, then develop the base car and the Berlinetta *off* the Z.

This change in concept marked a total break with tradition. Camaros of the earlier two generations had been engineered as the base version first, with up-option models derived later. Thus the Z-28, Berlinetta, the F41 suspension package, plus the older RS, SS, and Type LT were done almost as accessory packages.

I'll let Tom Zimmer explain. Zimmer, you'll remember, was the man basically responsible for the 1977½ Z-28's handling when Chevrolet revived the Z after its 2½-year hiatus. Tom also headed the engineering team that gave the 1982 Z-28 its ultimate handling.

"This latest time around," says Zimmer, "we were looking for a car that was going to be totally performance oriented. We designed for that from the start, not as an add-on option package. The third-generation Camaro has the handling characteristics that it does because we knew what we wanted going in. We were very, very concerned with such things as on-center steering preciseness, cornering capabilities, responsiveness, and predictability. We wanted a car that was quick; that would handle right up there with the best in the world.

"I personally set the lateral acceleration goal for our guys at the proving grounds," Zimmer continues. "I wanted them to shoot for [a lateral acceleration figure of] 0.90 g! Well, that's unheard of. You can't get that. The best we've measured for any production car is around 0.85 g. But we're right up there. The 1982 Z-28 has no trouble pulling 0.83 g, which is better than the Ferrari 308-GTB and the base 1981-82 Corvette."

The symbol *g*, by the way, stands for *gravity*. One g equals the force of gravity. The 1982 Z-28's lateral acceleration figure of 0.83 g means that when cornered to the limit, anything inside the car is being pushed toward the outside of the turn at a propulsion rate equal to 83% of the force of gravity. The driver, for example, is being shoved against the inner door panel at .83 g.

Zimmer's man in charge of ride and handling at the proving grounds was Freerk Jetze (Fred) Schaafsma. Schaafsma came to this country from Holland in 1962 at age 15, and he describes himself as a teenager who liked to take things apart to see how they worked. He graduated from high school in Royal Oak, Mich., and went on to General Motors Institute—GM's own engineering college—in Flint. Chevrolet Engineering became Schaafsma's sponsoring unit when he entered GMI in 1965, and in essence he's been with Chevrolet ever since.

"We were looking for a Z-28 that would surpass, from a handling standpoint, almost anything on the market," notes Schaafsma. "We felt it had to have lots of ultimate cornering capability, and one of the other things we decided on early was the Z's on-center handling characteristics. That's the preciseness of handling where most people tend to drive: going straight down the road. We aimed for immediate response to small steering-wheel inputs. We felt the car had to show its stuff there, too."

Backing up a bit, the F-Car engineers had to contend with the same front- versus rear-wheel-drive question that plagued GM's stylists. After the corporate Future Product Conference of May 9, 1977 recommended making the next-generation Camaro and Firebird front wheel drive, Chevrolet, Pontiac, and Engineering Staff all launched programs to study the feasibility of a fwd F-Car. X-Car development was entering its final stages, but finished X-Cars weren't yet available for evaluation. So the engineers initially used fwd imports to get a handle on state-of-the-art fwd handling.

The first corporate ride-and-drive to explore the possibility of applying fwd to the F-Car took place in Aug. 1977. This junket made its way through the back roads of Kentucky. Rides-and-drives amount to vehicle evaluation trips on which engineers (and

At one point, General Motors decided the next Camaro should be fwd, so work began on upgrading a Scirocco to handle like an F-Car. Ram at right examined VW's strut-tower stiffness to get a baseline for fwd Camaro handling.

sometimes designers and management) check out cars in actual on-the-road conditions. This particular ride-and-drive's purpose was to compare the capabilities of typical fwd cars against some of the world's best-handling fwd cars and also against the then-new (1978) Camaro and Firebird.

Included on the Kentucky trip were a turbocharged VW Scirocco, a pre-prototype GM X-Car, Honda Accord, Alfa Romeo Alfetta GT, Porsche 924, Pontiac Sunbird, a Firebird Trans Am with the WS-6 package, a Camaro Z-28, and a standard Camaro Sport Coupe.

Participants from Chevrolet were engineers Paul King, Tom Zimmer, Russ Gee, and Jack Turner. Bob Knickerbocker and a few other Project Center people went along.

Another ride-and-drive took place in Southern Michigan soon afterward. This trip included two Sciroccos (one stock, one turbocharged), a Renault 17 Gordini, an Audi 100-LS, Fiat 128 3P 1300, Ford Fiesta, Honda Accord, Lancia Beta 1600 HPE, plus a 1978 Z-28 and a '78 Trans Am WS-6.

Neither ride-and-drive reached any specific conclusions, but the engineers agreed generally that none of the fwd imports could match the handling and predictability of the 1978 F-Cars—not even those aimed toward the sporty-car market: the Sciroccos, Lancia, Saab, and the Gordini. In the Southern Michigan ride log, two terse statements stand out: "None of the example vehicles were acceptable to Chevrolet as future F-Cars," and, "Fwd cars did not display F-Car ride and handling characteristics or security feel."

Next, Chevrolet tried to *make* a fwd car handle to the standards of a Z-28. The idea was to see—as objectively as possible—whether and how much a fwd automobile could be improved.

"I was working for Jack Turner at the time," recalls Fred Schaafsma, "and I took time off from various other projects to become completely devoted to trying to make a fwd car handle up to our expectations. By looking at the front-end structure of various fwd cars—what capabilities you end up with by moving suspension components around, using different tires, wheels, and some of the roll-stiffness structure ideas—we were able to get the front-drive cars pretty good from an on-center handling standpoint.

But they just never came close to our expectations on ultimate handling. The cars never got to be fun to drive. They were always heavy on understeer. When you tried to work around it, they'd become non-linear and kind of tricked you. They wouldn't transition very nicely."

Schaafsma did most of this early work on a VW Scirocco. A similar Pontiac team under Norm Fugate tried just as hard to bring another Scirocco up to F-Car standards. Pontiac added a turbocharger to its Scirocco and, just before Christmas 1977, sent the car—along with a group of engineers and drivers—to Willow Springs Raceway in Southern California.

The Pontiac engineers wanted to compare what they considered the ultimate-handling fwd sporty car with the latest WS-6 Trans Am. Senior project engineer John G. Callies was in charge of Pontiac's Willow Springs venture, and he remembers it this way:

"Our chassis group had been working with this Scirocco. The car was modified to have our best thinking on fwd suspension. We had it at what we felt was max handling but not necessarily the best over-the-road ride. On top of that, we turbocharged the VW engine. We'd just come out with our WS-6 suspension package, so I trimmed the carburetion of a Trans Am with the WS-6 to give it the same acceleration as the turbo Scirocco. We set the two cars up so their 0-30-mph and 0-110-mph acceleration times were within a 2% variance. The idea was that, out of the turns, neither car would have an acceleration advantage.

"The test I set up," continues Callies, "included three professional race-car drivers and three good amateur drivers. The pros were Danny Ongais, John Morton, and Mort Kessler. Among the amateurs was Don Fuller of ROAD TEST Magazine.

"We went out to Willow Springs and ran a series of 10 laps with each of the cars. The overwhelming results were that the pro drivers could get closer to the T/A with the Scirocco than the amateur drivers could, but both amateur and profession drivers were running about 2.5 seconds faster around the track in the T/A than in the Scirocco."

By that time, Chevrolet and Pontiac engineers had become pretty well convinced that fwd was not the way to go. For example, F-Car Project Center head Robert H.

Ungainly Camaro pre-prototype simulated hatchback with hot-wire-bent glass attached to roof with crude hinges. Spy photographers believed production

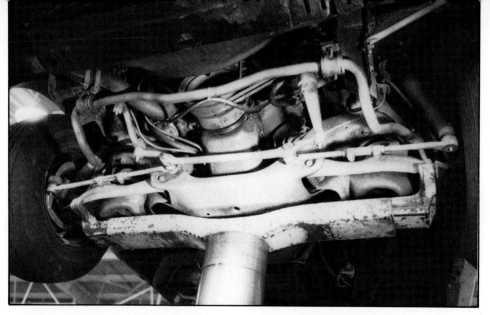

F-Cars would look like this. Front suspension cradle, hefty stabilizer bar, general steering geometry began to take shape underneath the pre-prototype.

Knickerbocker told me spontaneously, "I have yet to drive a fwd car that provides the type of feel that I think an F-Car owner is used to—the handling he would anticipate in a car he bought called a Firebird or Camaro."

Tom Zimmer likens a fwd "handling" car to a man who's trying to hold up a ceiling. If he can use both hands, he might stand a chance. If he has to use one arm, though, to support a bucket of paint at the same time, he's definitely handicapped. "Once you begin putting dual functions on one system, you reduce the system's capability to do either job 100%," Zimmer points out. He's talking about making the front tires of a car perform both propulsion and steering functions concurrently.

Fred Schaafsma adds, "My reaction, after months of trying, was that we just couldn't make the Camaro as a fwd car."

Yet some very level engineering heads and extremely qualified GM management people still held out hope for fwd. Commonality of parts with the X- and J-Cars became one good reason not to abandon fwd so quickly. Also, there was no doubt that an X- or J-based fwd F-Car would have greater fuel economy.

But one consistent and very strong voice in *favor* of rear drive belonged to F. James McDonald. Mr. McDonald at that time was a GM vice president in charge of a wide range of corporate activities, including car and truck, body and assembly divisions, electrical components, mechanical component groups, and service parts operations. From 1969 to 1972, McDonald ran Pontiac, and as the division's general manager he developed a great fondness for and a thorough understanding of the Firebird and Trans Am. Jim McDonald, who's now GM's president, never wavered in his conviction that a V-8 engine was absolutely essential to the survival of the T/A and also the Camaro Z-28.

"To me, the fwd/rwd decision boiled down to the fact that the Camaro and Firebird had been very successful, partly due to their styling but also because of their performance images—the Z-28 and especially the Trans Am," comments Mr. McDonald. "Performance is vital to those two cars. To me, that means a V-8 engine, and when you go to transverse fwd, there's no possibility of a V-8. You wipe it out. So I feel that was the deciding factor."

O nce GM's Product Policy Group gave concept approval to a new rear-drive F-Car on Feb. 22, 1978, most Chevrolet engineers breathed a sigh of relief. The program could finally move forward.

Bob Knickerbocker began immediately to build up his staff at the F-Car Project Center. He'd recently moved out of the Design Staff body room and into the GMAD building at GM's Technical Center in Warren, Mich. During its four years of existence, the F-Car Project Center would move (physically) no fewer than five times. And what began as a nucleus of three people would expand to 150.

"The project manager," says Knickerbocker, "goes to the various divisions, searches out the people he wants, and tries like hell to get them. The core Project Center group works for GM Engineering Staff; then most of the people who come in still get paid by their individual divisions or staffs, but they're centrally located, with central direction."

I told Mr. Knickerbocker that the F-Car seemed like such a fun assignment that it must have been easy to get good people. "It's true," he replied, "that I didn't have much trouble talking the *people* into coming, but I did have some difficulty getting their bosses to let good people go."

Members of the F-Car Project Center core group included Dan Agresta, who came in early as administrative engineer and later moved up to assistant chief engineer; Steve Major from Chevrolet took over as chief engineer after Bob Knickerbocker retired in Dec. 1980; Chevrolet's Norm Milostan became body systems manager; Pete Lupescu arrived from Pontiac as chassis systems manager; and John F. Harris served as structural systems manager.

At the height of its activity, the F-Car Project Center first occupied space at the Engineering Staff annex and then moved to the huge new north wing of the GM Engineering Staff building. Here, if you somehow qualified for a security pass, you'd enter as a visitor through what seemed like endless corridors. Finally you'd arrive at a great, brightly lit room filled with drafting tables.

All around this open space would be a perimeter of glass-walled engineering offices. Out in the middle, shirt-sleeved draftsmen would quietly be putting lines on paper, one man to a table. And inside the outer offices, engineers would be writing or meeting or

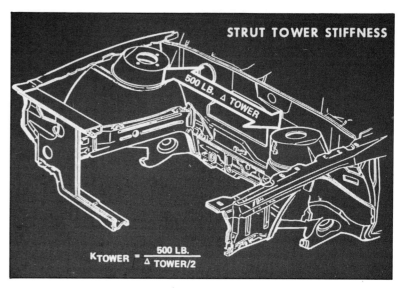

Recognizing that structure would be of paramount importance to Camaro's handling, Chevrolet set strut-tower stiffness goal of 30,000 pounds per inch,

again used a hydraulic ram (left) to test. By fabricating various gauges of tower cover plates (opposite, right), the engineers eventually met their goal.

talking on the telephone. There's an air of quiet urgency in the atmosphere—a rush.

In the center of the vast ocean of draftsmen, you'd see a large glass room, like an oblong island—the *mockup room*—filled with bucks and prototype components. Engineers and mechanics inside the jumbled but highly ordered mockup room would be poring over spec manuals or working to fit newly made pieces together. There'd be several engine bucks for fitting powerplants, routing wires and hoses, and making sure that engines could be worked on properly. Trunk and seating bucks would similarly prove out packaging in those areas. And you'd see actual cars in various stages of assembly.

I can't over-emphasize the importance of the Project Center as *the* focal point in the F-Car's creation. And while I did touch briefly on the Project Center's early role in Chapter One, I feel its later functions also need some explanation.

Basically, the auto divisions at the Project Center create the paper car. Every thread of every nut and bolt has to be preconceived on paper, decided upon, and carefully correlated with every other part. Without a paper car, there can be no mechanical car.

The Project Center, then, has three main functions: to coordinate, to schedule, and to ride herd on every conceivable detail of creating and bringing the F-Car to market. I'll let assistant chief engineer Dan Agresta fill us in on some of the inner workings of the Project Center.

"Our first job was to coordinate the objectives of the new F-Car. What was the third-generation Camaro going to be in terms of design features, components, size, shape, finances, market, and so forth? We pulled together what the body styles ought to be, component interchangeability, performance, fuel economy, and package size. After the divisional designers made preliminary drawings showing occupant and luggage locations, we began targeting costs and laid out the program schedule."

Eventually, the Project Center created the so-called *Program Content and Objective Manual*, a set of two large looseleaf notebooks that gave detailed descriptions and drawings of every component of the new car.

"The *Program Content and Objectives Manual*," continues Agresta, "lists the program objectives in generalities—such things as dimensions of the vehicle, aerodynamics and fuel-economy targets, structure and interior noise objectives, durability and

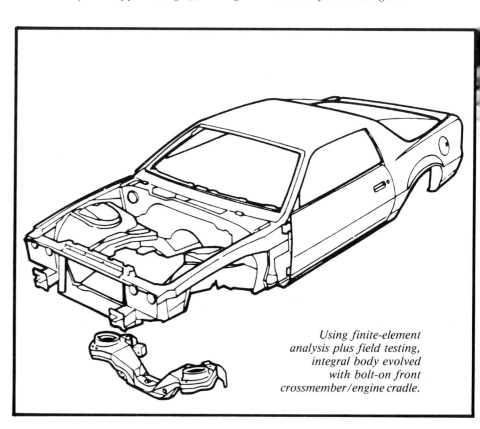

Using finite-element analysis plus field testing, integral body evolved with bolt-on front crossmember/engine cradle.

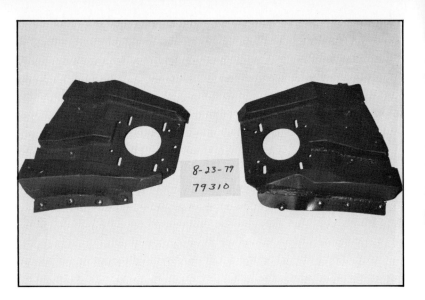

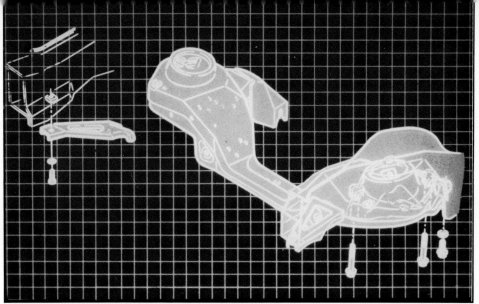

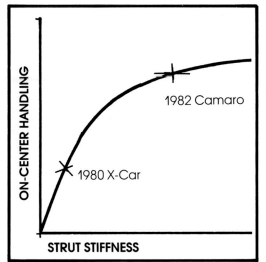

Camaro engineers began with X-Car's 20mm front strut rod but found it too limber for good on-center handling, went to 22mm rod, finally ended up with 25mm for a notable gain in precision.

Six bolts attach front crossmember (above) to main body section, while guide pins ensure precise location. This crossmember supports not only the engine but the front suspension and brakes as well.

Called a modified MacPherson front suspension, coils don't wrap around struts but rather stand between single lower A-arm and crossmember. Mercedes uses a similar design, as does Ford. It's lightweight, compact, and effective.

reliability goals, serviceability, the design validation program, corrosion objectives, parts commonization, startup and timing of the various phases of development, plus who's got what coordination responsibility from the divisions.

"Then in a second section, you'll see that as the car comes together, the parts and pieces are spelled out in excruitating detail. It goes from system to system by what we call UPC's [Uniform Parts Classification], with UPC 1 being the body, UPC 2 the frame, UPC 3 the front suspension, and so on down to UPC 15, which we call the 'junk

A drafting room the size of a football field dominated F-Car Project Center, in which ''paper'' Camaro was born. At one time, 150 engineers labored here.

As components were released for production, samples came to mockup room inside Project Center to be assembled into a car. Charts on wall show engines.

UPC' because it includes everything not spelled out in the previous 14 categories; things like paint, trim, accessories, and so forth.''

This UPC book is constantly being updated as parts and specifications change. Copies go out to everyone who has any hand in the program: people in manufacturing, procurement, assembly, serviceability, warranty, design, and various staff engineers in the car and component divisions.

''These books are put together here in the Project Center,'' Agresta points out, ''and one of the big advantages is that you get everyone looking at this car from the very beginning. Used to be, everybody had to wait until the design-coordination engineer got around to letting people know what he'd done after the fact.

''We're basically a communications organization,'' Agresta continues. ''We spend a large part of our Project Center lives attending meetings. We have three levels of meetings,'' and he showed me three different calendars, each filled to overflowing with a predetermined month of meetings. One calendar showed corporate meetings. A second calendar was for meeting with component manufacturing groups: the manufacturing managers from the various GM divisions. ''Monthly, we go to their meetings,'' Agresta told me, ''and tell them the current status of this particular car program.

''Then on top of that,'' notes Dan, ''another calendar schedules out the coordination meetings. These are individual meetings that take place every day, dealing with specific components. Here, for example, is the instrument-panel and console meeting, here's the corrosion control meeting, production validation meeting, bumper design, underbody coordination, serviceability, Fisher Body divisional meeting, and so on and so forth.''

Nor were even *those* the sum total of meetings. ''Every Monday we used to have a staff meeting, in which the systems managers reported on their areas of responsibility. They reported to us so we could get prepared for our management and corporate meetings. A Project Center is attending meetings. It's getting involved with the design coordination engineers so we'd know where the program stood from the financial point of view, in terms of manufacturing, assembly, and all the other disciplines. We tracked the car one way or another, and we reported on all this to corporate management.

''At the beginning of the Camaro program,'' concludes Agresta, ''we started off with three people. We eventually worked up to 150, and six months after the car came out,

we were back to three. Then we closed up the records and everybody received another, different assignment.''

The Project Center housed, of course, many Fisher Body, Chevrolet, and Pontiac engineers. Robert C. Stempel directed Chevy Engineering in 1977-78, followed by Lloyd Reuss in 1979-80, with Paul King taking over in 1981. Tom Zimmer worked directly under Reuss and later under King. Zimmer, as mentioned, was Leo Szady's boss, and Fred Schaafsma and Bob Haglund reported to Szady.

Schaafsma handled the handling, and he approached it from the hands-on end. Fred and his staff did their work at both GM proving grounds—the main one near Milford, Mich., and also at the GM Desert PG at Mesa, Ariz. Zimmer visited often and scrutinized intensely.

''One of the neatest things and part of the real fun and enjoyment of engineering this new Camaro,'' recalls Tom Zimmer, ''was sitting around with Fred Schaafsma and his development guys in the evening, talking about the car; talking about the kinds of things we thought it ought to do and, as we went along, formulating certain specific aspects of the personality and character of the Z-28.

''Even when they were working in Mesa, there wasn't a week that I wasn't out there. The routine...I'd leave on a Tuesday evening [from Detroit] and spend the next day in the car. Fred and the guys and I would sit around the campfire in the evening, shooting the breeze about what we wanted this car to do and how we were going to tune it this way or that. Then I'd catch the red-eye back to Detroit. But we'd shape and mold the car's personality as we went along.''

Zimmer and Schaafsma had become convinced of the adage ''handling via structure'' when they worked together on the Z-28's reincarnation for 1977½. It's long been recognized that a car won't handle if the body, suspension, and steering components are free to flex.

''After we finished the 1977½ Z-28,'' states Schaafsma, ''we started working on the 1978 Z, which had the soft front fascia. That really illustrated the effect of body structure on handling. When we put the soft nose on that '78 car, a lot of the metal that had

Spikey-looking dowels on gridded metal floor pinpoint positions where various components go during car's assembly in Project Center mockup room.

Using $75,000 handbuilt prototypes, Zimmer and Schaafsma's team worked out Z-28's handling first, then turned their attention to Berlinetta, F41, *and base car. This marked a radical departure from past practice, which developed the Z-28 as an option package added onto the basic Sport Coupe.*

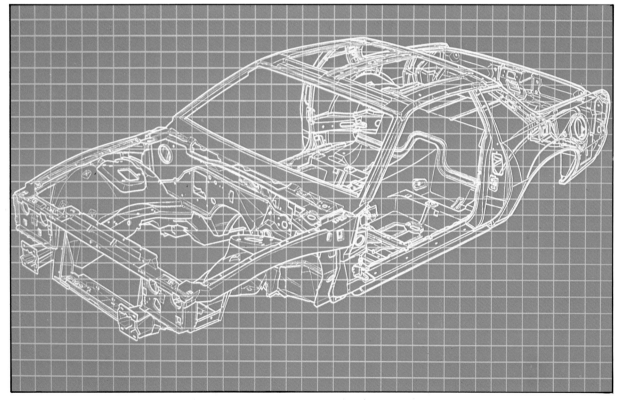

Vehicle Handling Comparison

Car	Under-steer (deg./g)	Roll gain (deg./g)	Steer-ing sen-sitivity (g/100 deg.)	Max. lat'l accel (g)
1980 Camaro Z-28	4.7	3.9	1.08	.73
BMW 320i	1.3	7.7	1.56	.74
Ferrari 308-GTB	1.8	6.1	1.38	.80
1981 Corvette	1.4	5.4	1.75	.81
1982 Camaro Z-28	4.0	2.9	1.30	.83
Corvette FE7	1.2	3.6	1.94	.84
Porsche 924	2.1	5.3	1.28	.85*

*Advertised
Source: General Motors Vehicle Research Laboratories.

Compare '82 Camaro's low roll gain (lean in turns) and high lateral acceleration with sports cars.

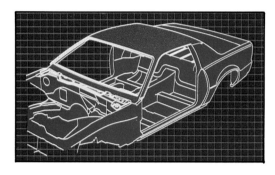

Computers played a greater role in creating the third-generation Camaro than in any previous GM car and saved untold thousands of engineering hours. One-piece outer roof (right) welds to cowl, B-pillars.

Zimmer jokingly set '82 Camaro's cornering goal at .90 g, which he acknowledged would be impossible. After hundreds of J-turns like this, done to evaluate minute changes in springs, shock valving, and tires, the production Z-28 recorded a consistent maximum lateral acceleration of .83 g (see chart).

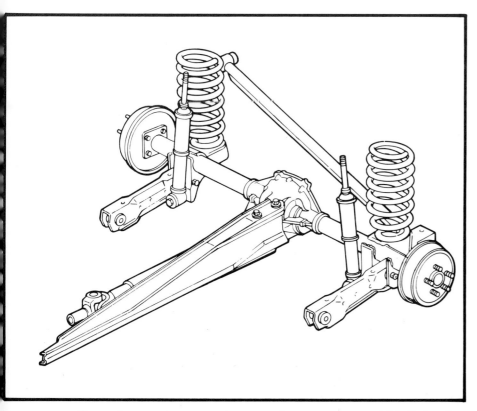

Camaro's new torque-arm rear suspension saves space, weight. Coil springs have no inter-leaf friction. Driving torque is absorbed by the trans mount.

Chevrolet engineer Fred Schaafsma (left) oversaw Camaro's handling, assisted by Larry Fletcher. Schaafsma subsequently took on '83 Corvette handling.

Several ride-and-drives during the prototype stage let GM management evaluate third-generation Camaro progress. Drives crisscrossed Arizona highways.

Much testing of Camaro prototypes occurred at GM Desert Proving Grounds near Mesa, Ariz., where durability and reliability runs went on for months.

To minimize interior resonance, acoustical engineers used sensitive microphones to pinpoint noise sources. Insulation could thus be put where needed.

Camaros and 1982 Firebirds often participated together in ride-and-drives, and rival makes went along, too. At other times each hit the road alone.

tied the front end together had been designed away. As it turned out, we had to go to some pretty fancy structural bracing, because at first the prototype Z wasn't handling as well in '78 as it had for '77½. It came as a big lesson.''

The 1982 Camaro, like the Scirocco and most contemporary cars, uses a unitized body. ''Body integral,'' as GM prefers to call unitization, was one of the original givens in the F-Car program, and that requirement never changed. ''Handling via structure'' therefore meant stiffening the unitized body until it became rock-solid.

I feel this needs some emphasis, because a lot of people aren't aware of the importance of body structure to the way a car handles. Structure turns out to be critical—more important, perhaps, than suspension, because without structure the suspension just flails around like wings on a jellyfish.

Explains Chevrolet staff chassis engineer Leopold T. (Leo) Szady: ''To make a car that'll have ultimate handling, the body structure needs to be very stiff and rigid. Anyone can build a car body that's lightweight, but the trick is to keep it from being flimsy like a matchbox. A matchbox moves when you twist or squeeze it. When you want a car to respond to steering-wheel movement, you don't want a whole series of structural flexing—a chain reaction where individual components move and swish around. If you want the whole car to respond promptly and exactly, you've got to make the body rigid—hold it nice and stiff.''

''How do you get good handling?'' asks Tim Zimmer. ''Mainly by getting the structure right. We designed this third-generation Camaro with the sort of structure that gives you great lateral stiffness [stiffness side to side]. We took the lateral compliance [movement] out.

''For example, you'll find that the cradle that holds the engine and front suspension to the body's rails doesn't have any rubber between the attachments. We knew going in that a metal-to-metal attachment would challenge us in terms of impact hardness and road isolation. How do you handle these? The best way is again via structure.

''Fortunately we knew how to build structure because of our experience with the downsized 1977 B-Cars and 1978 A-Cars. These have very well defined structures, and

one of the tools we used very effectively in all our programs was the computer. We set stiffness requirements for the F-Car in terms of torsional stiffness, bending, lateral compliances, and so forth.''

As in the styling area, computers played a tremendous role in speeding up and refining the F-Car's engineering process. Computer or ''math'' models—that is, precise computer programs that could be set up to simulate real in-metal cars—helped determine everything from body structure to engine placement, spring rates, and even such picky details as mounting the hatch striker in rubber to damp out a ''boom'' or resonance inside the passenger compartment.

Again, it might be appropriate to tell something about how these computers are used. Suppose you're interested in body structure. The characteristics of different types of commonly used metal components can be put into the computer as a series of numbers. For example, an I-beam of a certain size, weight, and strength enters the computer as one series of numbers representing its physical characteristics. Those numbers become the *math model* of that I-beam. Similarly, you can enter, say, three square feet of sheetmetal into the computer, along with all the characteristics needed to make that sheetmetal part of an inner or outer fender.

When you enter or program all the structural elements you think you'll need to ''make'' a car body in the computer—the beams, rails, sheetmetal, welds, fasteners, hinges, braces, reinforcements, etc.—you enter information about the actual physical properties of those elements, and you also enter ways to put them together. In other words, you could, for example, ''weld'' two ''metal'' I-beams parallel to one another, and you might end up with one double beam that's twice as strong as the single beam. Or you might find out that it's not twice as strong—or that it's three times as strong. Those are the sorts of facts the computer can give you.

That's how *finite element analysis*, as the engineers call it, works. They figure out engineering strategies on their computers the way you might play *Space Invaders* at your local pizza parlor. And just as you can see what'll happen if you ''drop a bomb'' or

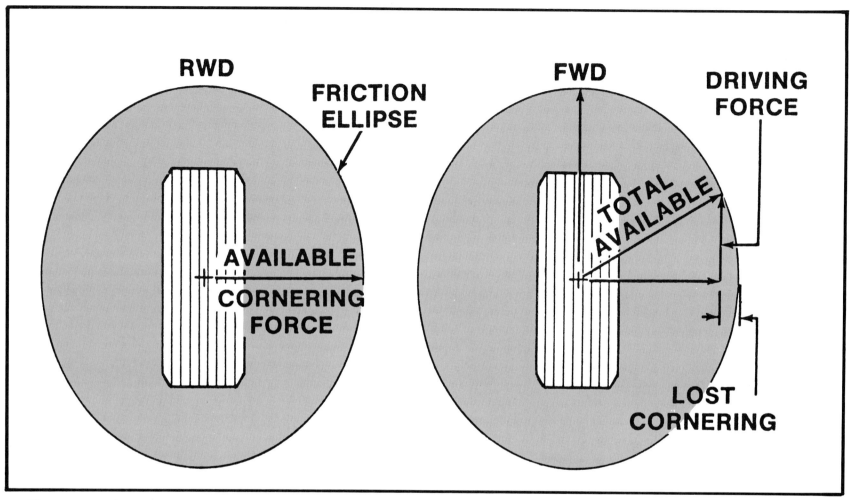

RWD

FRICTION ELLIPSE

AVAILABLE CORNERING FORCE

FWD

DRIVING FORCE

TOTAL AVAILABLE

LOST CORNERING

The reason rear-drive cars can out-handle fwd's can be illustrated by looking at their front-tire friction ellipses. The fwd vehicle has to devote a cer-tain amount of its tractive force to moving the car forward, so it can't give the front tires 100% of the adhesion needed to prevent side slippage.

"launch a missile" in a certain direction, the engineers can see what'll happen if they add a reinforcement to a rocker panel or use a heavier gauge of sheetmetal for a suspension strut tower. The computer principles are exactly the same. It's just that the engineering computer program is more complicated and comprehensive.

Several engineers shared responsibility for the new F-Car's computer modeling: Charles L. (Charlie) Potter at Fisher Body, John Frank Harris of GM Engineering Staff, and Mitchel C. (Mick) Scherba at the Project Center. These three—separately and together—created the finite-element models that determined the 1982 Camaro's structure and suspension system. Potter, Harris, and Scherba worked closely with Knickerbocker and Haglund at the Project Center and with Zimmer and Schaafsma in the field.

"In the very early stages of the component car," says Potter, "when we were talking specifications, definitions, and initial packaging, we used a very rough, coarse math model that we could put together in a hurry. We tried to discover the most efficient load paths so the car could stay light and still meet all the objectives for ride, handling, structure, and so forth.

"The front end of that new Camaro is unique because the underbody rails come back and nuzzle into the tunnel to form the support area for the transmission. Crossbars come across, tied to that from the rockers.

"We were initially of the opinion—once we settled on the modified MacPherson-strut front suspension—that the Camaro's strut towers should be kind of like the X-Car's. But it turns out that the F-Car's handling is so critical that that wasn't so. They had to be quite a bit stiffer. We built a very detailed math model of the whole front wheelhouse, the shock [strut] tower, and lower rail and did quite a bit of work on the local stresses and deflections of that area to arrive at the proper [metal] gauge to meet the handling targets Tom and Fred [Zimmer and Schaafsma] were asking for.''

Potter squeezed that early Camaro work into the more urgent business of finishing up the X-Car. That's also one reason he thought of using beefed X-Car front-end components. At that time, the F-Car was still destined to be fwd, so it seemed logical to just reinforce the X pieces to fit the F. But when GM decided to offer a V-8 and make the F-Car rwd, the whole program had to start over.

"We really had to scratch our heads and start in a new direction," Charlie Potter goes on. "Initially, the F-Car had been envisioned as a coupe, not a hatchback. But when we abandoned the 1980 L- and X-derived program and got into the '82 rwd car, Design staff came back and said HATCHBACK, which is a much harder body to do than a coupe.

"On top of that, they wanted the option of a T-top with that big glass hatch. Now at GM, we'd never done a T-top hatchback before. We've done it now, of course, and so has Datsun with the 280-ZX and Ford with the Mustang/Capri. But back then we knew we'd run into problems, because the hatch means you lose the structural reinforcement ahead of the trunk or behind the rear seats. Second, you also lose the bonded-glass backlight. Third, when you start taking a roof apart and try to put all that structure back into one central beam of the T-top, that's quite a challenge."

I asked Potter whether he could use the computer to tell whether it was possible to go ahead with the hatchback-cum-T-top.

"Oh, absolutely," he replied. "The rough math model we did in the beginning told us the construction was possible and also gave us the right paths for the body structure. Then as we got closer to release date and Design Staff gave us the outer skin configuration, we sat down and said, All right, now we'll build a finer, more concise math model, and we'll use that to tune in joint rates; that is, where the beams intersect, what bending rates they have, and how they deflect.

"That also became the model we used with Fred to tune the vehicle—to find beaming and torsional frequencies and to define those elements that had *nothing* to do with beaming or torsional frequencies or local modes, like floorpans, etc.

"Frankly," continues Potter, "The best use of a math model is to discover what you *don't* need in a car's body structure or suspension or whatever. Anyone can build car after car after car and finally find all the problems. But there's no way to quickly, effectively tell which gauges of metal are too thick and weigh too much and waste money and fuel *except* by running the math model through the computer.

"So what we did in both the pre-prototype and the prototype stages was to use the math model to: 1) identify those parts that didn't seem to have any effect on beaming or torsional frequencies or shake, and 2) identify which elements of the vehicle were sensitive to ride. We used both ends of that spectrum to put together a ride package.

"We actually ordered the shaped metal parts for such things as wheelhouses, strut towers, rails, crossmembers, and so forth from our prototype people. They made several parts of these items from thicker and thinner gauges of steel. Then, in conjunction with Fred Schaafsma and his ride-and-handling development team, we took all those parts down there to the Desert Proving Grounds in Mesa so we could sort through them to find the ones with high influence and low influence, as the computer directed us. By doing that, we were able to both tune the car properly and to achieve good stiffness for beaming and torsion. And we also managed to take weight out of the car at the same time."

Three stages of vehicle development usually precede the pilot production of any new automobile. First there's the *component car*, the second stage is known as the *pre-prototype*, and finally there's the *prototype*. Only the prototype looks like the final car—the others definitely don't.

Chevrolet chassis design engineer Tom Ryding, under the direction of Bob Haglund, began building the first component car or "mule" on Dec. 22, 1978. Between Christmas and the spring of 1979, when the pre-prototype phase began, several more component mules were built. They're called mules because, frankly, component cars never look much like thoroughbreds.

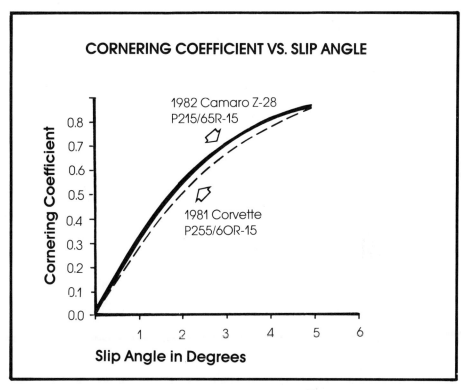

The 1982 Z-28's narrower Goodyear tire showed a higher cornering coefficient than '81 Corvette's which, up to that time, set the industry standard.

The main function of component cars is to give the engineers a chance to look into front and rear suspension systems, engine placement, weight distribution, tires, and brakes from an overall handling point of view.

Comments Fred Schaafsma: "It was with the component cars that we set specific targets in terms of rates for the strut towers and front suspension, steering gear, body rails, and so forth. That March, at the Desert Proving Grounds, we similarly established front and rear suspension geometry for the Z-28, the Berlinetta, and the base Sport Coupe."

Component cars were built up from H-Special (Monza) main body sections with A-Car (Malibu) front ends grafted on. "Ryding in essence cut the front end off the Monza and welded a section of an A-Car front frame onto the H-Car body structure," notes Fred Schaafsma. The front track, of course, was noticeably wider than the rear.

"We selected the Monza," adds Tom Ryding, "basically for two reasons. First, that car's rear suspension design was similar in concept to what the 1982 F-Car was going to end up with. Second, the distance from the driver's H-point to the rear axle was almost identical. We could also extend the front end forward by grafting on the A-Car frame section and end up with a vehicle that would have almost the same weight distribution as the new Camaro."

Chevrolet trucked that first component car from Milford to Mesa shortly after the beginning of 1979, "...and we had an engineering ride that March," continues Schaafsma, "that included Paul King, Tom Zimmer, and Bob Haglund. Pontiac had built up a similar component car under the direction of Bob Neuharth and Norm

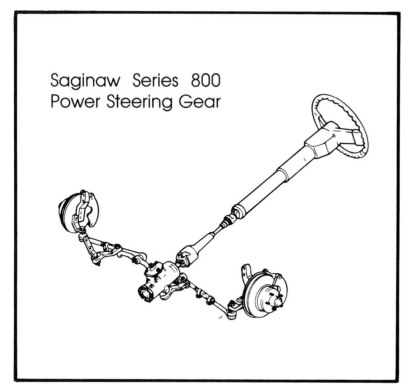

Saginaw Series 800
Power Steering Gear

All but base Camaros use recirculating-ball power steering, with Z-28 getting a fast 12.7:1 ratio plus limited boost to give driver more road feel.

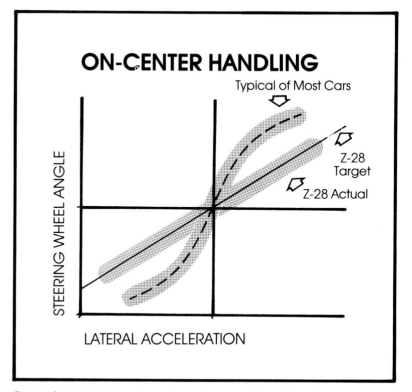

ON-CENTER HANDLING

Typical of Most Cars

Z-28 Target

Z-28 Actual

STEERING WHEEL ANGLE

LATERAL ACCELERATION

Camaro's on-center steering, where minor corrections take place, comes much nearer ideal (target) than most cars, which also have a larger dead band.

Fugate. We used that ride to establish where some of our concerns were. That was the first time, for instance, when we discussed going from the 205 tire to the 215. We then brought those cars back to Milford and did a lot of structural work—establishing structural stiffness and beginning to look at the front-suspension strut towers.''

Here's an example of how structural development and suspension development go together. It's impossible to work on one and not the other.

In the beginning, Chevrolet would have liked to use the same type of front suspension as on the first- and second-generation F-Cars; that is, conventional SLA (short and long arm). Trouble was, with the third generation's unitized body and bottom-loading engine, there was nothing really solid to attach the upper control arms to. Providing a hefty upper attachment would have added too much weight.

So after reviewing several other types of front suspension systems, the Chevrolet chassis design team gave the green light to a modified MacPherson strut. It's modified in that the spring, instead of encircling the strut high up, fits down on a lower control arm. In terms of weight and space, it's a much more efficient system and, as mentioned, the crossmember that carries it unbolts. That makes assembly easier in the plants because it allows bottom loading of the engine. It also simplifies removal and repair. Mercedes uses a similar system, as does Ford in its Fairmont-based automobiles.

One extremely important body area affecting handling was strut-tower stiffness. That plus the stiffness of the strut rod and the strut casing determined the effectiveness of the new Camaro's front suspension.

Based on computer modeling and early work with the Scirocco, Schaafsma's team calculated that they needed a strut-tower stiffness of 30,000 pounds per inch (ppi). ''We can measure that,'' says Larry Fletcher, a young engineer on Schaafsma's staff, ''by pushing between the two strut towers with a hydraulic ram. We apply a load, then measure it as we look at the strut tower's displacement. The number, we figured, needed to be 30,000 ppi per tower. That's what we have on the 1982 Z-28 now.''

During the component-car phase and also in the pre-prototype, Schaafsma's group fabricated various different strut-tower caps. These bolted or were welded to the upper wheelhouses. Eventually, though, the computer told him the ideal combination of strength and light weight to get the 30,000-ppi job done. So by the time he got to the prototype stage, the wheelhouse and strut-tower structure was pretty well set.

''Another area we looked at,'' continues Fletcher, ''was the strut itself. That was a new concern, because we didn't have much experience at that time with strut stiffness as it relates to a handling car. Early in the F-Car program, we started off with the X-Car strut, which was a 20mm rod. That wasn't stiff enough, so we went to a 22mm rod. The 22mm strut rod was actually released for production, but then we found that even that wasn't stiff enough, so we finally ended up with a 25mm strut rod.''

The strut itself is the same type as the X-Car's, but the Camaro's is considerably beefier. No parts interchange. The X's strut has a stiffness rating of 4500 ppi versus 7000 ppi for the F-Car. The X uses a 50mm-diameter strut with 2.4mm wall thickness, as against 54mm with a 3.2mm wall in the F.

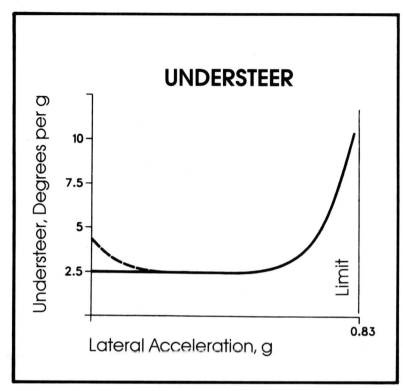

UNDERSTEER

Understeer, Degrees per g

10

7.5

5

2.5

Limit

0.83

Lateral Acceleration, g

Average American driver finds some understeer desirable. New Camaro's handling makes front tires lose traction before rear, but slowly, predictably.

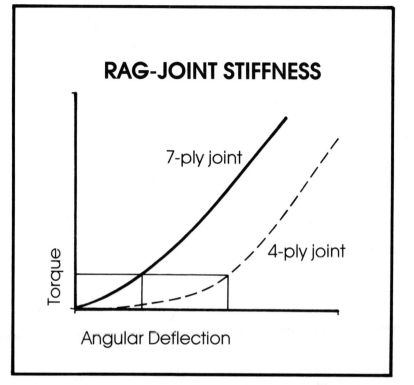

RAG-JOINT STIFFNESS

7-ply joint

4-ply joint

Torque

Angular Deflection

So-called "rag joint" at bottom of steering column takes up angular deflections. Z-28's rag joint has three more plies for greater steering precision.

The Camaro strut also uses a taller bracket with a reinforcement weld. In addition, the fluid, lip seal, and piston are all different, and perhaps most important, there's a ball-bearing mount up top that rotates with the strut rod as the front wheels turn. This ball bearing is unique to the Z-28 and Berlinetta. It makes steering lighter and gives a more rigid upper mount.

By the way, this entire front strut system, which was developed for the Z-28, is also used under the other two new Camaro models—the Berlinetta and the base Sport Coupe. Springs, shocks, and bushings are different, but you'll find identical struts in all third-generation Camaros.

The new Camaro's lower control arms, which began life as grafted-on A-Car parts in the component cars, remain modified A-Special (Monte Carlo) units even today. The metal stampings are slightly changed, with different steering stops, bump stops, a little more meat, and no hole for the shock. The Camaro A-arms also have a larger cage for the rear bushing, and the stabilizer-bar limiting grommets are polyurethane for better roll control.

To let Fred Schaafsma elaborate: "When you're doing handling work, the lower control arm really does nothing more than react to centrifugal force, which is lateral. So consequently, during cornering you experience lateral loading.

"What you'd like to do is get that path as directly into the structure as you can. Our 1982 Camaro control arm is now very similar to the A-Special's, which is similar to the

1981 F-Car's and the 1981 B-Car's. These are all derived basically from the 1970½ F-Car front suspension. Anyway, one bushing—the front bushing—counteracts those lateral loads. The front bushing ends up being your handling bushing, and it has to be quite hard.

"The rear bushing, though, can be soft—for fore-and-aft impacts. It's about a 90/10 relationship; that is, the hard front bushing takes care of 90% of the lateral loading and 10% of the ride. The softer rear functions 90% as a ride bushing and 10% for handling. It became very important to get that sorted out, particularly for a car like the Z-28. Once we figured out the relationship, it gave us the ride we wanted in a very, very good-handling vehicle."

The Z-28's front bushing comes by its larger size because it's taken directly from the B-Car. It's not the stock B-Car bushing, though, because it's made of a stiffer rubber. And the lower control arms also contain special, low-friction Kahr-Lon balljoints.

"The thing I want to get across," Schaafsma points out, "is that our toughest job was developing the handling of the Z-28. That was really Number One. Then Number Two was trying to get the ride out of the Berlinetta. The F41 suspension package...I wouldn't suggest that it was unimportant, but we could almost decide in an afternoon what we wanted to try, based on figures and valving and what we'd done to the other suspension systems."

Zimmer and Schaafsma aimed for a lateral acceleration figure not of the 0.90 g that Zimmer mentioned tongue in cheek but for a more realistic and very respectable

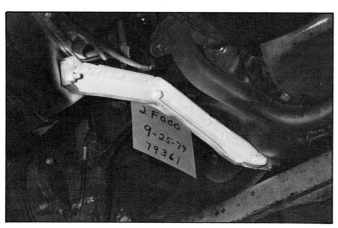

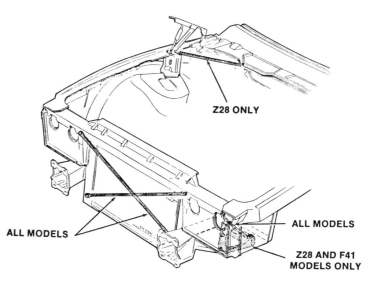

FRONT SHEET METAL BRACES

Z28 ONLY

ALL MODELS

ALL MODELS

Z28 AND F41 MODELS ONLY

While body structure provides basic inflexibility, some bracing became necessary to aid handling. Photos at left depict early experimental braces. In its final form, the Z-28 took on only minor gussets at steering box and to compensate for strength lost to duct holes in cowl for air conditioner.

"greater than 0.80 g." That's the number entered in the Z-28's original target specs.

The third-generation Z-28, as you know, ended up with a lateral acceleration of 0.83 g, which is the limit of tire adhesion; the point at which tires begin to lose traction and start slipping sideways. At that point, the engineers decided they wanted to have slight understeer that was as linear as possible. In other words, the front tires should lose their grip before the rear ones do, and this forward-plowing motion ought to be predictable and constant. The car's tail shouldn't try to come around (as oversteer), nor should the car change capriciously from understeer to oversteer in the middle of a fast sweeper.

A great number of cornering and handling tests were done in all phases of development—component car, pre-prototype, and prototype—at Black Lake on GM's Milford Proving Ground. Black Lake isn't a lake at all, though; it's a virtually flat, 59-acre patch of asphalt. When it rains on Black Lake, the surface looks so much like deep water that ducks occasionally pancake on it. A car can spin out on Black Lake—wet or dry—without any danger of tipping over or hitting anything. The sorts of ongoing tests done at Black Lake included lateral acceleration, response times, on-center handling, steering friction, side-slip angle, body roll angle, and tire testing.

Tire tests, in fact, resulted in a brand-new set of tires for the Z-28. When initial specifications had been drawn up for the Z, they called for tires of 78 and 70 aspect ratios—quite tall and narrow for a handling car. In the component-car phase, around Feb. 1979, the Z-28 tire was going to be a P205/65R-15. "When we got the cars on the

road, though," mentions Schaafsma, "we determined that there wasn't going to be enough load capacity. It looked like we were going to run out of tire. On that basis, we decided to go to a P215/65R-15 for the Z-28 instead of the 205."

GM, as you know, sets various standards for all the tires it buys. It's a system started by Edward N. Cole in the early 1970's. The stickiest tires yet developed by or for General Motors have traditionally been used on Corvettes: their optional Goodyear P255/60R-15's on 8-inch rims.

The 1982 Camaro Z-28 tire uses 35 psi inflation pressure for lower rolling resistance. In casting about for the ideal handling tire, Schaafsma's group and GM's Vehicle Handling Lab tested dozens of brands, both domestic and imported, in various sizes and tread patterns. The contest came down to the Pirelli CN-36, a VR215/60R-15, versus Goodyear's P215/65R-15. The Pirelli actually showed a trifle more adhesion, but it was down in terms of on-center steering response.

And it turns out, the 1982 Z-28 actually beats the 1981 Corvette in the categories of cornering coefficients, and it meets all of GM's stiff Tire Performance Criteria for durability, wet and dry traction, rolling resistance, high-speed performance, and trueness.

Another critical aspect of handling involved getting the new Camaro's steering system right. Like the body structure, steering has to be made totally tight and un-

Berlinetta's much softer ride leads to some body lean on high-speed turns, but tire adhesion is still more than adequate for all normal driving situations.

compliant. Any flexing or bending has to be engineered out. Schaafsma's team, under Zimmer's watchful eye, again concentrated on making the steering as responsive as the rest of the car.

Chevrolet looked at rack-and-pinion steering for the third-generation Camaro and rejected it. Engineering director Paul King explains, "We opted for the conventional recirculating ball type of steering, and the Z-28 will have Saginaw's 800-series steering gear with a 12.7:1 gear ratio. That's the fastest ratio of any Camaro to date and a very good gear.

"I don't want to sound defensive, but we didn't see rack-and-pinion as the panacea for all steering ills. We can do a good rack and pinion; we can do a lousy rack and pinion. BMW and Mercedes help support our use of recirculating-ball steering, and we feel that steering excellence comes more in the execution than in the type."

Fred Schaafsma goes on to say that, "...steering system stiffness is extremely crucial. You look at the compliance of a system, its ride-steer capabilities, and also at its frictional characteristics. Now ride steer is something you want to use, particularly on a car like the Z-28. But it needs to be tailored.

"If you have a rack-and-pinion system," Fred continues, "with what we call an *end takeoff*, then because the tie-rod ends are very short you're liable to end up with severe ride steer.

"So we said, Well, maybe we can have a center-takeoff rack and get out of that problem. But now all of a sudden you've got long, long tie rods, which tend to be compliant. *And* they're running right through the body structure—right where you *want* structure. If you put the steering arm up high on the strut instead of on the knuckle, you have to worry about the distance between the steering arm on the strut and the tire on the ground. That distance is so great that you'll likely end up with a lot of torsional strut compliance there. Also, the mounting of the rack to the body gets tricky. You've got to have it in a spot that's stiff enough, but then that might add to the input of noise and vibration.

"Meanwhile, with the recirculating-ball system, you have very low frictional characteristics plus the use of conventional parallelogram steering linkage, which lets you do a lot more tailoring. And you don't have to go as far away from the tires with your steering arms."

Another area of steering compliance came at the so-called "rag joint." That's the fabric coupling atop the steering gearbox that takes up shaft angles. Conventional rag joints are 4-ply, but the handling engineers felt this wasn't stiff enough. So they developed and ordered up a 7-ply rag joint, which is now standard on the Z-28 only. "It's another effort at fine-tuning the steering," says Schaafsma. "The 7-ply rag joint gives us the on-center crispness we wanted. No other car uses it, not even the Trans Am Firebird."

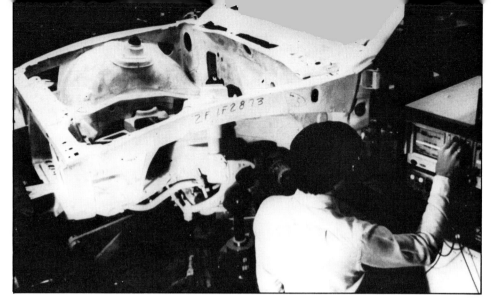

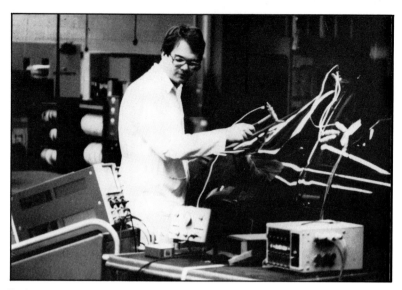

Cycling machine shakes front-end structure to see how much stress the metal and welds can take. Vibration cycles can be set for strength and amplitude.

Technician uses acoustical hammer on Camaro rear glass to see if he can induce "boom." Much acoustical work was done in laboratory and by computer.

Such details were worked out over all three stages of vehicle development: component car, pre-prototype, and prototype. Pre-prototype construction began in Apr. 1979 and put all the decided-upon elements in place: the final but unrefined types of suspension, a close approximation of the floorpan, the general underbody structure, the right brakes, engines, cowling, etc.

But the pre-prototypes still looked nothing like an actual F-Car. They were essentially cobbled early-production X-Cars that had been converted to rear-wheel drive. Comments body structure engineer Charlie Potter: "The pre-prototypes were made from Buick Skylark coupes. Doors and tail lamps were recognizable as Skylark, and so was the front half of the roof, but the quarters were all wrong, and the cars looked just awful."

Pete Lupescu adds that among the reasons for choosing X-Car bodies for the F-Car pre-protos: 1) the rocker sections were similar to the eventual F, 2) overall width likewise, and 3) a liftback could easily be simulated in the Skylark to approximate the '82 Camaro's.

Lupescu estimates that 12 pre-prototypes were built in all—six representing Camaros, six as Firebirds, of which two each were used in handling work and the rest went into fuel certification, emissions, structures, barrier testing, etc.

Pre-prototype work progressed both at Milford and Mesa. "We took the cars to Mesa that fall and had a ride for Paul King, who at that time was chief engineer of Chevrolet passenger cars," states Schaafsma. "Tom Zimmer and Lloyd Reuss were on that ride, too, and everyone came away very pleased.

"Of our three pre-prototypes used for ride and handling, one had all the features of a Z-28, one was an early version of a Berlinetta, and the third went for structural development. The Berlinetta got extra attention, because with the hatch and the bolted-on front crossmember, we were asking ourselves, Can our ride and quietness goals be achieved? We did a lot of work toward that, and with the proper isolation, insulation, and structure, we worked it out." And as a ride target for the Berlinetta, Schaafsma mentions using a BMW 528—the big BMW had the ride, steering, handling, and road feel that Chevrolet considered appropriate for the Berlinetta.

A lot of thought went into the F-Car's rear suspension, too, of course, and much of this work happened at the pre-prototype stage. The earlier component cars—those with the H-Special main body section—happened to use the torque-arm type of rear suspension; the same type finally selected for the new Camaro and Firebird. But that had almost nothing to do with *why* the ride-and-handling engineers chose the torque arm for the third-generation F-Car.

Pontiac has design responsibility for all corporate rear suspensions.* Bob Knickerbocker told me that, "Pontiac built up several cars, and so did Chevrolet, and those had various designs of rear suspension systems. Most were laid out by Pontiac engineers. In some cases Chevrolet made its own proposals. Then we evaluated all these and pulled the facts together and presented them at our monthly chief engineers' and managers' meetings."

Knickerbocker goes on to explain that Pontiac first considered carrying over the same sort of leaf-spring rear suspension as on the second-generation F-Car. This, though, brought with it a heavy weight penalty.

Second thoughts ran to a 4-link coil setup, which pares weight but takes up a lot of space. The gas tank and rear seat locations didn't leave room for the upper links. Nor is there enough structure near the hatch floor to hook them to. You also run into power-hop and noise-isolation problems in a unit-bodied hatchback with 4-link rear suspension, as GM found out with the H-Special. They changed that car from 4-link to torque-arm rear suspension in 1975 and gained not only space but silence, axle control, and handling as well.

Other types of rear suspension talked about for the third-generation F-Car included the Corvette's independent system, various types with Chapman struts, a deDion rigid, a rigid torque arm, rigid torque tube, and rigid leaf. These were all compared in a rating chart, which listed packaging, ride, cost, manufacturing considerations, and weight. In the end, the torque arm won out.

Bob Haglund sees it this way. "The torque arm packages nicely. The longitudinal member attaches to the differential case and runs up to the transmission. Because it's so long, it lets you take the axle torque and resolve it as a relatively small force. You also get a chance to feed that force back directly into the powertrain, not into the body, so

---

*Just as Chevrolet's design responsibility extends to all GM front suspensions and brake systems.

you have extra isolation for less noise." All in all, the torque-arm setup does everything it's supposed to.

Throughout the development program, Schaafsma and his team constantly worked on front and rear shock valving. Ride-and-handling engineers use special take-apart shock absorbers for this work. "We have a whole big bin of different valves, orifices, and springs for blowing off the valving.... So in a matter of 20 minutes, you bring the car in, put it on a lift, unbuckle the shocks, dump out the fluid, remove and re-install valves, put back the shocks, and you're out on the track again. Typically during a day, you might try as many as 10, maybe 12 shock valves." Final shock determinations are subjective, with the engineers simply feeling which settings they like best. Shock valving has relatively little to do with handling, but it's crucial to ride.

Another area where you have to cut and try is in rear-suspension geometry. I asked Bob Knickerbocker whether this meant building, rebuilding, and re-rebuilding the same car several times. "To an exacting degree," he answered. "Rear geometry had to be changed to everything it possibly could be. That's the job of the development engineer. He moves everything a quarter inch at a time, up and down, back and forth, until he finds the optimum. Not much of that work can be done with the computer. A good suspension designer can lay out the points, and a good development engineer builds them into the car and experiments and experiences."

Camaro prototypes, which finally looked very much like the final 1982 car, started being handbuilt in Mar. 1980. Body panels were stamped with low-volume Kirksite dies, and while as many components as possible came from the proper sources, most were pre-production samples.

The arrival of prototypes gave everyone a chance to do major and minor revisions as needed, to blend in that very important ingredient, *pleasability*, and to wrap up the finer points of detail engineering. Fortunately, no major changes were necessary, but an awful lot got done in the detail area.

Structures specialist Charlie Potter told me about an early glitch that showed up in the huge glass backlight. Prototype production samples from PPG and LOF looked fine until the first time someone tried to slam a hatch shut. When he pushed down on one corner, the frameless glass bent about 4½ inches before the hatch would start down. It didn't break, but the bending looked awful. Solution: increase the thickness of the glass from 5mm to 6mm. That solved *that* problem but created another.

Charlie Potter explains: "The 6mm backlight contributed to a phenomenon called *boom*. It gave a low, rumbling vibration at certain car speeds. This was actually caused by the high-pressure tires. To get around the boom, we developed a super-slick rear lock striker mechanism that's mounted in rubber and is tuned to the hatch. By design, the rubber mount lets the hatch move slightly."

Another bit of engineering finesse came in the Z-28's gearshift knob. Fred Schaafsma reports, "Design Staff had come up with a knob that we felt wasn't comfortable, so I had our machine shop make me a round ball. This ball was 2¼ inches in diameter. The interior guys weren't too happy, but they went along. In June, we had Chevy's general manager, Bob [Robert D.] Lund and then-director of engineering Lloyd Reuss [pronounced Royce] out for a ride. I was riding with Reuss, and he says to me, Boy, I sure don't like that ball; it's way too big; it ought to be smaller.

"Well, the 1981 ball had been two inches in diameter, so everybody chimed in, Let's make it two inches again. But I said I thought two inches was too small. We ended up making it 2 1/8 inch. Now I know this sounds picky, but the 2 1/8 ball was it! It's fantastic. In fact, I like it better than the 2¼-inch knob."

Considerable detail work went into the bolt-on front crossmember, too. The person directly responsible for the final job was Chevrolet design engineer Don Beane. He mentions that the initial thought was to adapt something like the first- and

Extremely accurate half-scale clear plastic model of Camaro body helped engineers find stress points. These show up as rainbow patterns on color film.

second-generation Camaro's "wheelbarrow" subframe, heavily bushed in rubber. But that wouldn't work for a number of reasons, the most important being weight.

"We finally came up with the crossmember as it is now—the engine cradle that also carries the suspension lower control arms. We did considerable finite-element analysis and lab testing on mounting this crossmember, seeing how to attach it so it stays attached. Originally we just bolted the top surface of the crossmember to the body rails. We put access holes in the lower surface and drove these relatively short bolts up into the body. But we didn't get enough stretch in our bolts to maintain the clamp force we wanted. Short bolts don't stretch enough, so if there's paint between the joint surfaces, the paint will wear, and the bolts relax. We ended up putting long, tubular spacers inside the crossmember and using six long bolts instead of four short ones."

Another good idea from Beane's group was the use of welded-in dowels to locate the front crossmember. There's one dowel on each side that matches a corresponding hole in the body. "The crossmember uses these dowel pins so we can maintain good cross-car relationships from a suspension standpoint. Originally we were going to use loose pins, similar to the body-drop method on the second-generation Camaro. In that car, we used to just locate the cradle and take the pins back out. But we had some access problems with the '82 Camaro, and then, too, we also worried about the cars when they needed repairs or servicing. How would a bodyman or mechanic ever put the crossmember back the way it ought to be? So we put these dowels right into the crossmember itself," explains Beane.

Such detail engineering and fine tuning continued in the prototypes right up to the point of pilot production. Design and development work never stops, but it does move from stage to stage. □

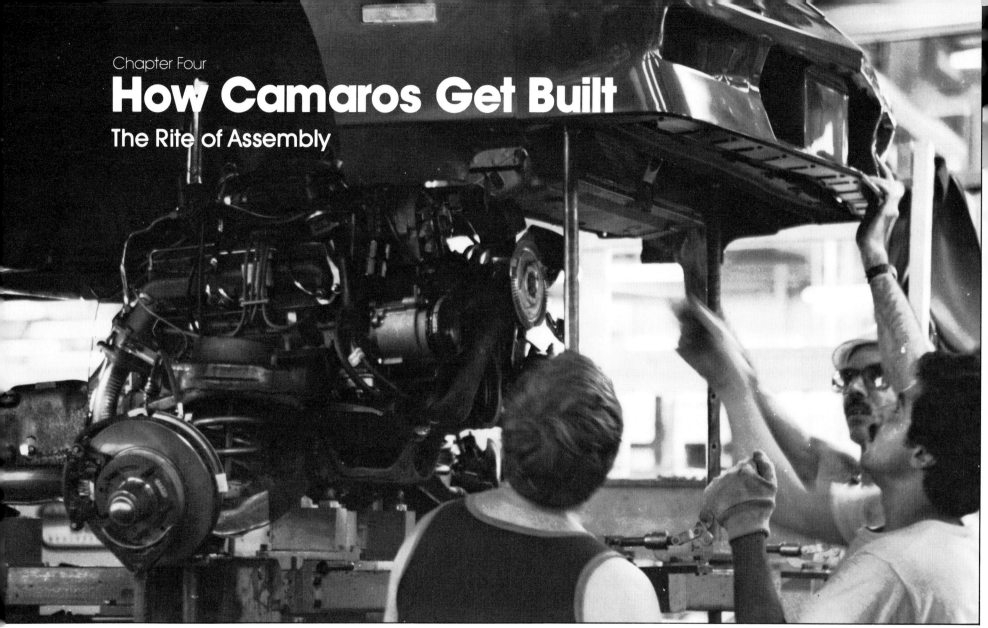

Chapter Four
How Camaros Get Built
The Rite of Assembly

All third-generation Camaro engines load from the bottom. This prevents damage to upper painted surfaces. Engines can be removed either from top or bottom.

PILOT PRODUCTION FOLLOWS the prototype stage and, just as vehicle engineers use prototypes to fine-tune the cars themselves, production engineers use "pilot" to work out kinks in the assembly process.

F-Car pilot production began in late May 1981 and continued through July. There were 100 bodies made, and in all, 89 pilot models were assembled: 51 Camaros and 38 Firebirds. The Camaros were put together in all three flavors and as many different op-

tion and decor combinations as possible. The 89 handbuilt pilots reflected standards of fit and finish that would later be duplicated in the two F-Car assembly plants at Norwood, Ohio and Van Nuys, Calif.

Pilot production serves a number of purposes. "The objectives of pilot," says production engineer Norm Milostan, "are to make certain that the parts are going together properly and that they look the way they should—that the car's appearance is right. Are

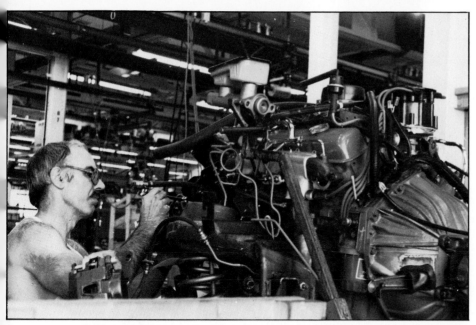

Bottom loading permits drivetrains to be assembled entirely out in the open before installation. Brake master cylinder and power accessories are load- *ed onto engine, then transmission, brakes, driveshaft, axles, and exhaust system are attached. Photo sequence shows pre-production pilot assembly at Flint.*

the parts being assembled in the right order? Can the build be speeded up or improved by changing the order of assembly? Can the cars be taken apart again by service mechanics? And do the numerous tools, jigs, fixtures, robots, welders, automatic tolerance-checking machines, and finishing processes turn out the quality of cars that Chevrolet expects?''

Pilot assembly is the same process you'll find later in the plants, but on a miniaturized scale. The major GM divisions involved in F-Car assembly are Chevrolet, Pontiac, Fisher Body, and GMAD (General Motors Assembly Div.). That's true for pilot production as well as final assembly. In addition, components and parts are also supplied by GM's supplier divisions—Delco, Harrison, Inland, Packard, Saginaw, Rochester, Guide, Hydra-matic—and by hundreds of outside suppliers.

For the Camaro, Chevrolet's responsibility is to subassemble and supply front-end sheetmetal back to the cowl; also the instrument panel, brakes, and certain powertrains. Pontiac subassembles and supplies the rear axle, fuel system, and the 4-cylinder engine. In the pilot program, Fisher Body provides the main body section components and is responsible for seats, hardware, and trim.

GMAD takes care of final production assembly and oversees all General Motors assembly plants. F-Car plants, as in the past, are located in Norwood, Ohio, which is surrounded on three sides by Cincinnati; and Van Nuys, Calif., a suburb of Los Angeles. Subassemblies arrive at Norwood and Van Nuys from Fisher (body and interior parts), Chevrolet (front suspensions, major brake components, some engines), Pontiac (the Iron Duke Four, rear suspension systems), plus other GM divisions and outside suppliers.

Before assembly starts at Norwood or Van Nuys, though, pilot production takes place in Detroit and Flint, Mich. Fisher Body starts the pilot process at its Detroit Central Plant 21, at the corner of Piquette and Hastings in downtown Detroit. Here Fisher assembles all the black metal, builds up the main body sections, and paints and trims them. Bodies are then trucked to GMARC—the General Motors Assembly Research

Center—in Flint, where they're joined by the divisional subassemblies for the final pilot build.

I should mention that the Chevrolet-supplied subassemblies are produced in three plants owned by the division: Chevrolet Metal Fabricating, which makes up the front-end components; Flint Engine, which builds powertrains; and Flint Pressed Metal. These three Chevrolet subsidiaries supply parts not only for the Camaro's pilot and final production but for all cars to which Chevrolet contributes. Pontiac, by the way, owns a similar set of plants that turns out Pontiac-supplied parts and subassemblies.

One unusual but by no means unique aspect of the Camaro's assembly process is the bottom loading of its engine and transmission. Instead of dropping the powertrain down into the hood cavity as in most cars, the Camaro's comes up through the bottom. It's subassembled in the plant and mounted on the front crossmember, which forms a sort of cradle. The engine can be final-assembled out in the open this way, without workers having to lean over fenders.

Observes Bob Haglund: ''Bottom loading helps get a high quality of fit and finish. We attach the fenders and hood and process all those parts through the painting stages along with the body. Imagine the same car with the hood, fenders, and radiator support installed and painted. If you now drop the engine and trans down from the top, there's a danger of messing up the paint job.''

What about the repair mechanic? Can he unload the engine up through the top? ''He can,'' answers Haglund, ''or he can take it out through the bottom. If he bottom-unloads, he has to support the body, take out the six crossmember bolts, and he then lowers the whole powertrain to the floor.''

General Motors has always taken pride in its quality, but quality gets even more attention now than in the past. As part of Chevrolet's quality program, engineers like Fred Schaafsma, Bob Haglund, Dan Agresta, and others—people who aren't directly involved in the assembly process—have traveled to both Norwood and Van

Nuys to talk to the workmen who do the actual assembling: to explain what the finished cars should look and be like, what they're intended to do in terms of ride and handling, why it's important to understand what distinguishes a Berlinetta from a Z-28. It's a process of explaining not only *how* a car goes together but *why*. And while GM has undertaken such programs before, never have they been so extensive nor intensive as with the current Camaros.

In addition to getting assemblers involved and interested, General Motors—or more specifically Fisher Body, Chevrolet, and GMAD—has developed a number of assembly-plant checking fixtures. These checkers assure fits and tolerances to a precision that human inspectors sometimes miss. The checking fixtures don't replace inspectors; they're intended mostly as backstops. And while inspectors look at every car, the checking fixtures might look at one or two per shift to see if there's a trend away from spec.

Checking fixtures are tried and tested during pilot assembly, then are moved to the plants at Norwood and Van Nuys. GMAD is responsible for designing, installing, maintaining, and for using these fixtures. Other fixtures, though, like fender checkers, are the responsibility of the divisions.

"Chevrolet, for example, has two sets of fixtures," says Norm Milostan. "First, a fender fixture checks the detail of the fenders themselves. Then second, there's a GMAD fixture called the C-55 that's been evolved for this new Camaro. The C-55 not only duplicates checking the fender, but it also checks the periphery fit to adjacent components—the hood, the door, and the front fascia.

"These fixtures use templates or gauges that bolt into place. A solid steel piece simulates the door and another one simulates the hood. Then, in addition to the templates, the fixture also uses feeler gauges to check clearances. These have tolerances of half a millimeter."

One C-55 fixture stays in Flint, at Flint Fabricating, and duplicates go to each assembly plant in Van Nuys and Norwood.

Another fixture, called CIMMS (for Combination Inspection and Metal Match System), aids Fisher Body by checking the full body structure. "There's a pointer on a surface plate," explains Norm Milostan, "and the operator uses pre-set fiduciary marks to locate the body in space. The pointer rides on a trammel, with dimensional readouts. The operator can pick any spot and tell you what that spot should read and what it does read. If the readout varies from spec by a set amount, the operator recommends adjustments or the inspection of specific parts."

On 1982 and later Camaros, virtually everything that's exposed to road salt or the elements comes in for some form of rust protection. In fact, third-generation Camaros are among the best-protected cars in the world today—on a level with Volvo (see chart, page 56).

Zincrometal is a type of sheet steel that has four coatings of zinc-rich primer baked onto its inner surface. Rust often happens from the inside out, and Zincrometal guards against that. Outside surfaces, of course, are protected by paint. (Zincrometal is a product and registered trademark of Diamond-Shamrock Inc.)

Galvanized sheet steel is another rust protector that the third-generation Camaro uses extensively. Galvanization, as you know, coats steel with zinc, and this can be done either electrolytically or by immersion. Some of the Camaro's structural pieces, like the body rails, are entirely galvanized.

The Camaro's exhaust system is corrosion protected, too, by making the exhaust pipe and catalytic converter casing of stainless steel and by using aluminized steel for most of the rest of the system.

Plastisol, used to prevent stone chips on exterior surfaces, coats all lower sections of rockers, fenders, and doors. Special hot waxes cover the inner top corners of the cowl, and aluminized wax is sprayed into inner fenders, rockers, and doors. Extra paint film covers the front toeboards of all Camaros—an area that tends to collect salt and moisture from passengers' shoes.

And some parts of Camaros simply can't rust. The Z-28 hood, for example; the front and rear body facias; the round fuel-filler door and fill cavity; the windshield trim—all

For pilot assembly, bodies were put together at Fisher Body Plant 21 in downtown Detroit, then trucked to over Flint. In all, 89 pilot Camaros were built.

One purpose of pilot assembly is to work out the processes to be used in the actual production plants—in this case at Norwood, Ohio and Van Nuys, Calif.

Coil springs have to be positioned fore and aft before the drivetrain can go in place. Rear half of exhaust system, though, has already been installed.

Workmen are about to bottom load Z-28's drivetrain. Next step is to fasten both front suspension struts and buckle up the transmission crossmember.

A pilot Berlinetta gets pinstriped. Technician applies pinstriping tape by first wetting surfaces, laying on the tape, and finally forcing out all air bubbles.

these are made from urethanes, SMC, and plastics. These plastics not only resist corrosion, but they save weight as well.

The way Camaros are being painted these days marks another departure. The routine differs from Van Nuys to Norwood, but here's a rundown.

First, I should mention that the GMAD plant at Van Nuys has increased its body shop, trim area, engine assembly area, and final assembly area by nearly 122,000 square feet to accommodate the third-generation F-Car. And Norwood has added a whopping half million square feet, much of it devoted to an all-new paint shop that incorporates a state-of-the-art *turbo bells* spray system.

At both plants, bodies are painted before any trim, software, or running gear go into the cars. The paint process begins with a thorough cleaning operation that removes all oils, grime, solder, etc., not only from outer surfaces but inner ones as well.

The body passes through a high-pressure water wash, then gets a detergent and high-pressure bath before an inspection and manual cleanup. The paint shop then gives the body a solvent wipe, a detergent soak, and an 8-stage clean-and-phosphate treatment. This includes washing with a strong alkaline cleaner, rinsing with hot water, going through a mild alkaline cleaner, another hot-water rinse, a zinc phosphate dip, cold-water rinse, chromic acid rinse, and finally a de-ionized water rinse.

"At that point," says F-Car Project Center systems manager for corrosion and durability, Allan P. Whittemore, "when the body comes out of the clean-and-phosphate facility, it's ready to accept what we call *cathodic elpo*. That's an electric-deposition dip primer."

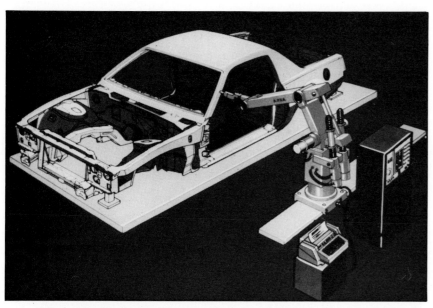

This is one of several checking fixtures that tests trueness of body openings during assembly. It matches what the probe "sees" against data in a computer.

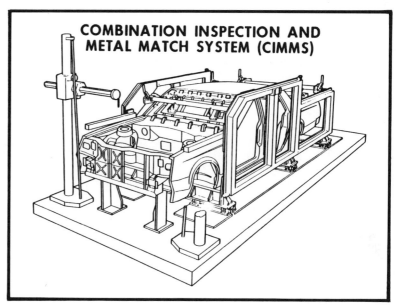

Not every car gets the once-over from Fisher Body's CIMMS checking fixture, but enough do so it can catch any trend that moves away from spec.

Cathodic elpo, instead of being sprayed on like a conventional primer, is deposited on the metal electrolytically, like chrome plating. The entire body is submerged in a huge vat or trough. The cathodic elpo has been positively charged, with the metal car body taking on a negative charge. All air bubbles are allowed to escape from the body so that there's nary a nook or cranny that the elpo doesn't reach.

Cathodic elpo is applied to all F-Cars in both plants, followed by a conventionally sprayed primer-surfacer. At this stage the actual paint-application processes begin to differ. Van Nuys uses the same final finish system that it's had for years, namely waterborne enamel that's applied with automated sprayers.

In Norwood, though, a new paint process called *turbo bells* has been installed. This is a process developed by the Ramsburg Corp. The paint itself is a high-solids, solventborne enamel, and it's applied with turbo bells.

Turbo bells are basically bell-shaped sprayers that incorporate high-speed (30,000-rpm) turbines. These turbines spray out a cone-shaped, atomized, electrically charged fog of high-solids enamel. Again, the car body carries an opposite charge, and the paint solids are attracted as in electrolytic plating. The solventborne paint consists of 44%-55% solids, and solids are the part of the paint that forms a coating on the car. The solvents are merely carriers that eventually evaporate.

To meet emissions standards, the Norwood turbo bells system has to come up to so-called "waterborne equivalency." That means that air quality with the solvent has to be as good as that with the waterbase paint used in Van Nuys. To meet waterborne equivalency, Norwood incinerates the evaporated solvent in burning stacks. This plus the use of the turbo bells and the high-solids enamel itself keeps air polution to a minimum.

The turbo bells system was tried initially on pilot-production models. Since Norwood's cathodic elpo dip wasn't yet ready, pilot cars were trucked to Van Nuys for the elpo application, then shipped to Norwood for painting with turbo bells. By the time 1982 production began at Norwood, though, everything had been set up, including a new clean-and-phosphate facility and a lengthened cathodic elpo tank.

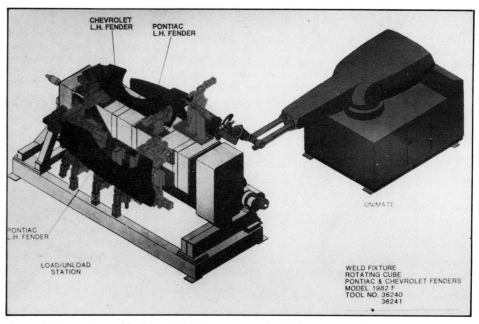

General Motors Assembly Div. uses many automated welders in both of the F-Car assembly plants. This one welds three Camaro or Firebird fenders at a time.

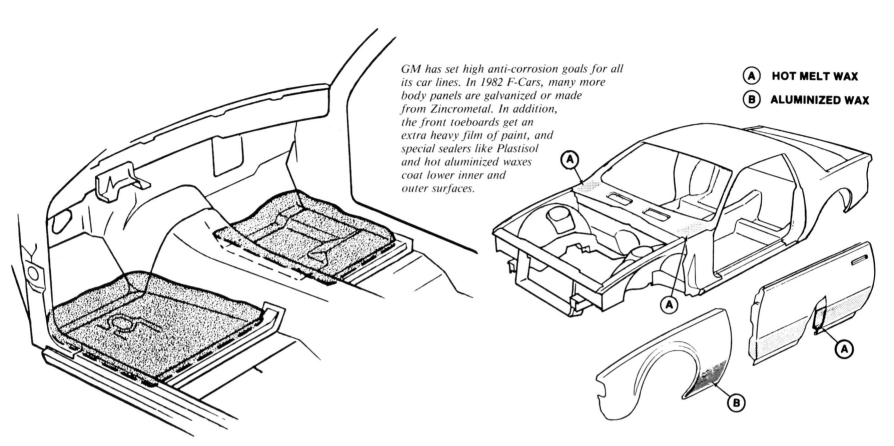

GM has set high anti-corrosion goals for all its car lines. In 1982 F-Cars, many more body panels are galvanized or made from Zincrometal. In addition, the front toeboards get an extra heavy film of paint, and special sealers like Plastisol and hot aluminized waxes coat lower inner and outer surfaces.

(A) HOT MELT WAX

(B) ALUMINIZED WAX

ANTI-CORROSION SEALERS

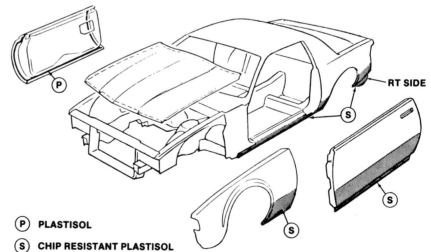

(P) PLASTISOL

(S) CHIP RESISTANT PLASTISOL

Winning the Battle Against Rust

Body Panel	1981 Camaro	1982 Camaro
Front fenders	Zincrometal	Zincrometal
Rear qtr. panels	Zincrometal	1-side galvanized
Doors	Zincrometal	1-side galvanized
Rocker panels	plain steel	2-side galvanized
Underbody rails	plain steel	2-side galvanized
Deck/hatch lid, outer	plain steel	Zincrometal
Deck/hatch lid, inner	plain steel	1-side galvanized
Rear end panel	plain steel	2-side galvanized
Rear compt. pan	plain steel	2-side galvanized
Fuel tank straps	plain steel	Zincrometal
Hood hinges	plain steel	2-side galvanized

This is one of the very first 1982 Berlinettas assembled. It temporarily took on a twin-TBI hood. All pilot-built Camaros were used for testing and durability.

Full-scale production of 1982 Camaros began at Van Nuys on Oct. 12, 1981 and at Norwood exactly two weeks later, on the 26th. Chevrolet general manager Robert D. Lund had hoped back in Dec. 1980 that the first 6000 Camaros produced on assembly lines should all be in one color (either silver or charcoal) and similarly optioned. This didn't happen, of course.

"The purpose would have been twofold," Mr. Lund told me. "First, in our quest for the very best quality we can build, if we repeat the process initially several thousand times, we're going to learn to produce a very good car. Second, I reasoned that by putting the same car out in large quantities, when people saw them on the streets, they would recognize them more quickly. The car would have more impact that way." It's an intriguing idea.

The first cars off the Norwood and Van Nuys assembly lines—like all 89 from pilot production—went to the various GM divisions for durability testing, emissions certification, photography by Chevrolet's sales staff and the Campbell-Ewald advertising agency, and for export to overseas divisions to modify for their local markets. □

Chapter Five

Engines for Every Energy

Two Hot V-8's, a new V-6, and the Camaro's First Four

When you order the optional twin throttle-body-injection V-8 (left) for the Z-28, you also get the lightweight SMC cold-air hood with NACA ducts (above).

THIRD-GENERATION CAMAROS offer three basic engines in four renditions. First there's the Pontiac-supplied Iron Duke Four, which began life as the original Nova powerplant back in 1962. It's been vastly improved and re-engineered since then, its latest innovation being to replace the carburetor with throttle-body injection (TBI). This 2.5-liter (151-cid), 4-cylinder engine comes as standard equipment in the base Camaro Sport Coupe.

Next, there's the 2.8-liter (173-cid), Chevy-built, 60-degree V-6 that began life in GM's X-Cars. It's been revised from transverse to longitudinal, and we'll see in a moment what that involved. The V-6 serves as the Berlinetta's standard engine and is optional in the Sport Coupe.

Finally, you can get the Chevrolet 5-liter (305-cid) V-8 in two versions: carbureted and injected. With the Quadrajet 4-barrel carburetor, it's the Z-28's base engine and

can be ordered optionally in the Sport Coupe and Berlinetta. In its injected form, the 305 becomes optional in the Z-28 only and uses two TBI units set on an aluminum crossram manifold—a very sophisticated system shared with the Corvette. I'd like to talk about all four engines, starting, naturally, with the twin-TBI 305 for the Z-28.

Chevrolet's chief engineer for engines and components, Russell F. (Russ) Gee, explained to me how the Z-28's new Cross-Fire Injection system came about.

"I moved from Pontiac to Chevrolet on Jan. l, 1979 and, in the middle of that month, a group of us had a brainstorming session on several vehicles. We sat down in my office and analyzed what we should be doing for the 1982 Camaro Z-28 and the 1982 Corvette.

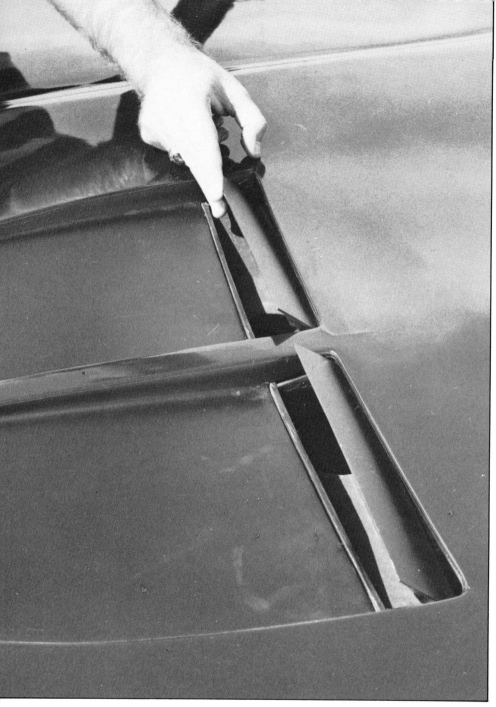

When driver floors the accelerator, throttle-position sensor signals TBI's electric control module (ECM), which opens cold-air inlet flaps via solenoid.

"We'd been challenged by management to come up with a unique engine for the Z-28. Years ago, back at Pontiac, I'd been involved in developing the old Tri-Power setup—the triple 2-barrel setup where you have one small carburetor in the middle of the intake manifold and two larger 2-barrels on the ends. I was really fond of that. We did a lot of work on it back in the GTO days under Pete Estes.

"What I particularly liked about the Tri-Power system was that you or your wife could drive around town five days a week and get excellent fuel economy with that very small center carburetor. Then on weekends, you'd floor the other two carbs and you had a real triple 2-barrel gangbusters engine.

"So when we sat down for this brainstorming session in my office," Gee continues, "it looked like we had three main alternatives available to us. One was to use a single 2-barrel TBI system like the 1980 Cadillac. The second was the one I introduced, namely three staged single-barrel TBI's in a row, like the old Tri-Power. And the third was a ram-tuned intake manifold with two electrically controlled carburetors on it—an update of what the Z-28 had used so successfully back in 1968-69 for SCCA Trans Am racing.

"We worked these three programs out in the laboratory for some time. When we tried to combine the three single-point TBI's, though, it became evident early in the program that synchronization would give us some headaches. The triple TBI setup really wasn't in the cards.

"As you'll recall, Chevy's success with mounting two carburetors on a tunnel-ram manifold got them outstanding power, so we built on that idea. We married the concept of putting two TBI units on this ram intake manifold, and we've come up with what I feel is a very, very strong, unique powerplant. It has great airflow capacity and power performance. We also have the capability of tuning the Z-28 to give very acceptable fuel economy."

To recap the TBI program's chronology briefly: Serious work began on the system in Feb. 1979, with initial specifications going to Rochester Products Div. that June. Chevrolet and corporate managers took their first ride in a twin-TBI vehicle in Aug. 1979. That December, Chevrolet received corporate approval on a twin Cross-Fire TBI system for the 1982 Z-28.

In Jan. 1980, Rochester agreed to manufacture completed dual TBI assemblies. GM decided at that time to have all corporate throttle-body components share the same machining lines. Crossram manifold castings became available in March, and by May 1980, Chevrolet had a Camaro prototype running with the new twin throttle-body induction system. It performed even better than anticipated and, by Apr. 1981, was turning 9-second 0-60's with the automatic transmission and 8.5 seconds for the 4-speed stick. A durability prototype completed a 50,000-mile test in Feb. 1981 and, by early summer, Chevrolet engineers finished emissions and fuel-economy tuning on the TBI 305 V-8.

Chevrolet engine engineering chief Russ Gee, incidentally, has an identical twin brother, Ray, who's an engine engineer with Cadillac. Cadillac pioneered the use of TBI on 1980 Sevilles and Eldorados. Basically, throttle-body injection is *not* a complicated system; in fact, once you understand the fundamentals, you'll see that it's simpler than today's electronically controlled carburetors.

Throttle-body injection isn't port fuel injection in the traditional sense. TBI doesn't use high-pressure pumps, complex fuel-distribution metering, expensive plumbing, or cantankerous injector nozzles at each cylinder.

Think of the throttle-body unit as a carburetor with the top part missing. The choke, air horn, venturis, float chambers, and all those upper-level jets and passages are gone. What's left is the throttle-body: the bottom plate with the throttle butterflies. But above that plate there's a solenoid-activated nozzle valve that can be opened and closed electromagnetically. Electrical impulses open and shut this solenoid at very high, precise rates and durations. You can think of it as a controlled vibrator.

Fuel at 10.0-12.4 psi pressure passes by the solenoid. As the solenoid pulses open and shut—and it does this once with each engine firing—gasoline escapes at a metered rate. It passes down into the throttle bores, at which point the fuel spray mixes with air in the same way it would mix inside the venturi of a carburetor.

Pressure in the TBI system's closed-loop fuel lines is supplied by a 2-stage, twin-turbine electric pump inside the gas tank. In the Z-28's dual TBI loop, the "master" TBI unit contains a pressure regulator. The master TBI stands farthest from the pump, with fuel passing through the "slave" on its way to the master. The master's regulator serves both throttle bodies, holding pressure at a constant 10 psi. If pressure builds up beyond 10 psi, a bypass in the regulator opens up and shunts fuel back into the tank.

The 10 psi in the TBI system is higher than what's normal in a conventional carburetor fuel line (6-9 psi), yet it's considerably lower than the 39-79 psi in port fuel-injection systems. That's important because in a 10-psi fuel loop you don't need the expensive lines and connections so vital to a leakproof port fuel injection system.

What actually determines how much fuel comes out of the solenoid nozzle valve? Again—electronic impulses. These electronic impulses are controlled by a microprocessor—a small computer that's tucked up behind the passenger's side of the instrument panel—which is why there's no glovebox in the Camaro's dashboard.

For the twin-TBI 305 V-8, you'll find two computer-controlled outputs—one for each TBI injector. Four-cylinder Camaros use a single TBI, and for those there's only one computer output. These on-board computers are also called *electronic control modules*, or ECM's.

The ECM takes information supplied to it from various sensors. It analyzes that information and, based on its analysis, tells the TBI exactly how much fuel to release. Sensors check manifold absolute pressure, engine coolant temperature, throttle position, road speed (mph), engine speed (rpm), and they also determine barometer from

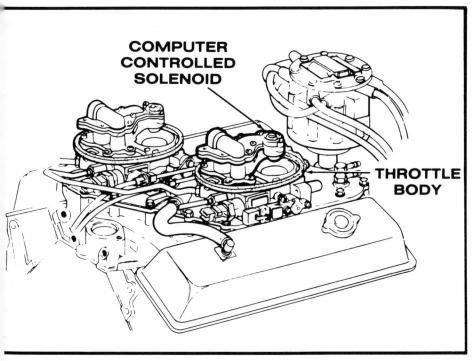

COMPUTER CONTROLLED SOLENOID

THROTTLE BODY

Visualize the Z-28's optional twin TBI system as dual carbs with the float bowls and upper sections removed. Fuel under pressure escapes when valves

open and shut very rapidly. Valves are solenoid-operated and controlled by ECM. Left TBI feeds right bank and vice-versa, hence the name Cross-Fire.

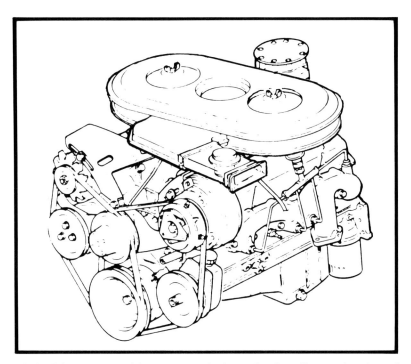

ECM (right) senses and interprets engine's needs, then dictates duration of each pulse and how wide the solenoid valve should open. At idle, pulses are *short and valve gap narrow. When driver demands full power, valve may stay fully open. TBI also does away with conventional choke and accelerator pump.*

manifold absolute pressure. Each sensor operates independently of all others. The ECM then electronically times or pulses each solenoid.

In the Z-28's crossram setup, the two TBIs' individual solenoid valves are pulsed alternately to coincide with the engine's firing order. In other words, the left-hand TBI supplies the right bank of cylinders, and the right TBI feeds the left bank. The banks fire alternately, bank to bank, so that's how the TBI's meter fuel—TBI to TBI, back and forth. Thus the term *Cross-Fire.*

The ECM-determined pulses are timed to engine speed. They're slowest and shortest at idle. As rpm picks up, so does the rapidity of impulses to the solenoids. Then, depending on load and other conditions, the fuel bursts might become longer in relation to engine speed. At full throttle, the solenoids can hold the injector nozzles open for maximum fuel flow.

In the Z-28's twin TBI system, each throttle body has a diameter of 1 13/16 inch. Directly underneath each throttle body, there's a *distribution plate* (also called a *swirl* plate). These distribution plates help mix the fuel and inrushing air, yet they're not restrictive and actually increase rather than decrease horsepower.

Several advantages accrue from the use of throttle-body injection. Fuel metering becomes extremely precise, so you use gasoline more efficiently than with a carburetor. Ignition timing, too, can be more carefully regulated electronically to control detonation, so the engine's compression ratio can be higher (9.5:1 in the TBI V-8 versus 8.6:1 for the carbureted 305). That again makes for greater fuel efficiency, which translates into more horsepower and more miles per gallon.

TBI systems need no choke, because the ECM is programmed to compensate for cold

starts by changing the fuel/air ratio. Nor do you need an accelerator pump to give that quick (and sometimes wasteful) squirt of gas for rapid acceleration. Again, the ECM senses throttle position and meets the need with the appropriate fuel/air mixture.

Further, the ECM incorporates an emission-control function. Anti-pollution devices on electronic carburetors have gotten very complicated of late. Electronic carburetors also use ECM's, but the TBI's ECM updates eight times faster in sensing the data and then metering an engine's fuel/air needs.

Then, too, there's a self-diagnostic function in the TBI system's ECM. The ECM can tell a mechanic what's wrong with itself or with the rest of the system. And even if the ECM goes haywire out on the road, there's a so-called *failsoft* backup that takes over so the engine doesn't quit completely. A special circuit comes into play and controls fuel delivery and ignition advance.

This failsoft system is not so sophisticated as the ECM's regular program, but it does provide fuel pulses to cover engine starting, idling, and normal running. You can at least limp home if your ECM fails.

According to Roland S. (Rollie) Taylor of GM's Rochester Products Div., which supplies TBI's for the Camaro, "Throttle-body injection was originally thought of back around 1970. We tried it for just a few weeks at that time, but it didn't seem practical because, in those days, emission laws didn't require the use of electronic controls. We could meet smog standards with relatively simple carburetors. So we couldn't justify the extra cost of a TBI at that time.

"However, when closed-loop technology came along to meet the government's ever stricter emission standards, that opened the whole field of electronic fuel injection, TBI

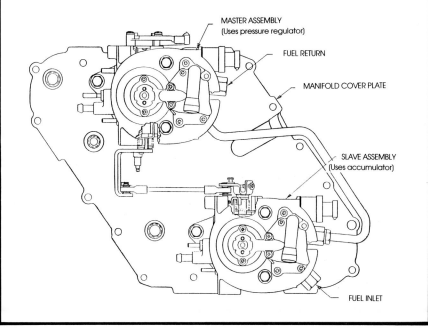

MASTER ASSEMBLY
(Uses pressure regulator)

FUEL RETURN

MANIFOLD COVER PLATE

SLAVE ASSEMBLY
(Uses accumulator)

FUEL INLET

Twin TBI uses master (left) and slave assemblies. Fuel under 10 psi pressure enters slave first, then circulates through the system and moves on to the

master, where a regulator assures constant pressure to both units. At low engine rpm, fuel not needed for power enters return line, goes back to tank.

included. We'd developed closed-loop carburetors, which became tremendously complex—electrical and mechanical controls for the idle system, off-idle, part throttle, the choke function, etc. Some were even outside the scope of electronic control. For example, a large, high-performance, staged carburetor with primary and secondary barrels—when you got to high altitudes, you had to control not only the primaries but also the secondaries for emissions.

"Port fuel injection," Taylor goes on, "tends to be expensive and also complicated. The man who brought TBI along and made it practical is Lauren L. Bowler, an engineer with our Powertrain Project Center. He did the TBI for the 1980 Cadillac and also worked on the ones being used on new 4-cylinder and V-8 Camaros. He delivered a paper to the Society of Automotive Engineers on the subject back in Feb. 1980 [SAE paper 800164]. What results from Bowler's work is a versatile, simple system that the average mechanic can cope with."

Throttle-body injection, by the way, is used only on Camaros sold in the United States. Canadian and overseas versions all use carburetors.

I asked Russ Gee whether Chevrolet had considered turbocharging or supercharging any of the third-generation Camaro engines. He answered this way:

"We have a unique advantage at Chevrolet. In my area, there's a group working under our chief performance engineer, Vince Piggins. These people look into concepts for the future. Vince's group is outside the production engine area, and they've got a turbocharger or supercharger program going for every powerplant Chevrolet builds. So yes, we've considered turbocharging and supercharging. I've been a real fan of turbocharging...."

"As for superchargers, they have the advantage of running at much lower rpm than turbos. Turbochargers run in excess of 100,000 rpm, while superchargers turn at engine speeds or slightly above."

Pontiac, of course, had offered a turbocharger on its Trans Am V-8's of 1980-81. Initially, Pontiac planned to continue the turbo option for 1982. Firebird planners, though, decided to go with the same engine lineup as in the '82 Camaro, especially since Pontiac was no longer manufacturing a V-8 of its own and would have to share the small-block Chevy anyway.

Chevrolet's engineering director, Paul King, answers the question of turbocharging with these words: "We thought about turbocharging and rejected it. At the time of the third-generation Camaro's development, Pontiac and Chevrolet were both heavily involved in looking at turbocharging. We knew Pontiac wanted to keep the turbo for the '82 T/A—and that remained the plan until mid-May of 1981. We were deciding whether to use some form of their turbo system, but we concluded it would be more cost-effective and better for our car overall to go to a little higher compression and TBI. We were after the immediate throttle response and knew we wouldn't have any trouble matching the top-end power of Pontiac's former turbocharged V-8.

"Of course," King continues, "we could turbocharge our TBI Z-28 engine and take another step up. That's not completely out of the question. And turbos might be available in special packages. Yenko's been working on turbos and special configurations, too."

I asked several Chevrolet engine engineers what they felt the aftermarket performance potential of the twin TBI V-8 might be. What, in other words, can the hot rodder do

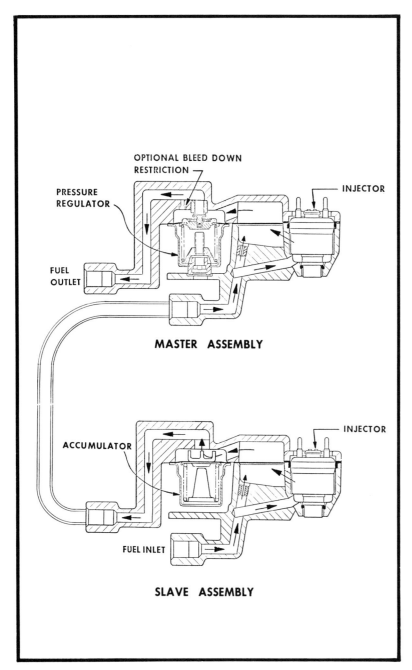

Schematic shows direction of fuel flow. Accumulator prevents gasoline from syphoning back into the tank, and regulator smooths and maintains pressure.

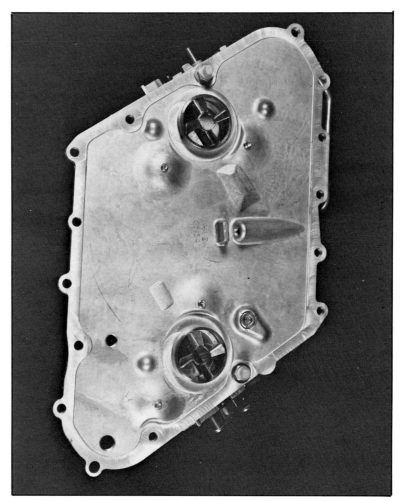

Swirl plates in bottom of manifold cover incorporate fans that help atomize fuel. Fans are turned by the inrushing mixture, do not act as superchargers.

or buy to draw more horsepower from the Camaro and Corvette twin-TBI fuel system?

They generally agreed that modifications *are* possible but not simple. Most felt it would take a total package approach, not just re-programming the ECM or somehow modifying the TBI nozzles or bores. It's possible for some clever Silicon Valley entrepreneur to re-do the ECM chip, and Chevrolet's Roger Dye told me back in Aug. 1981 that, "...I wouldn't be surprised if somebody somewhere hasn't already purloined a cookbook that tells where the chip's addresses are...." By "addresses," he means the chip's locations that control spark, fuel supply, emissions, torque-converter clutch engagement, etc.

The total package approach, though, would necessitate a higher compression ratio plus freer breathing via bigger valves, relieved heads, a smoother exhaust system that might use two monolith catalytic converters instead of the stock single, and perhaps a

train. The 5.7-liter [350 V-8] was probably the largest engine that got serious consideration. But once you accept the small-block V-8, it could have gone up to 400 cid.

"The other thought was—and since we were peering into unknown market conditions, we wanted to be flexible—to include different powertrains. We couldn't afford to use just a performance engine, nor could we put ourselves into the position of planning for economy only. The extremes, though, fell away—the 5.7 V-8 and the smallest Four."

The original range of engines for the 1982 Camaro included the carryover 4.4-liter V-8 (267 cid). That engine, though, came so near in performance to the V-6 that Chevrolet decided to drop it from the Camaro and now offers it in only a few cars.

Adds Al Rasegan, "The exhaust system also came under revision for the TBI to work. Basically, the entire system allows the engine to breathe better, so it became an important part of the whole."

Both 305 V-8's—the carbureted version and the TBI—use identical exhaust manifolds, takedown pipes, and tailpipes as far back as the catalytic converter. Outer overall pipe diameter for most of the exhaust system is 2.25 inches. Explains Chevrolet assistant staff engineer Lawrence M. (Larry) Weathers, "At the converter, we do differentiate, because we use a monolith catalytic converter on the twin TBI and a beaded-type converter on the carbureted 305. We went to the monolith for the TBI V-8 because of its naturally lower restriction."

All exhaust tubing back to the converter on both V-8's is of double-walled stainless steel, with an 0.17-inch airgap between tubes. The airgap helps keep heat in. That way, the converter comes up to temperature faster from cold starts.

Both 305's, as mentioned, use identical exhaust systems back to the converter. Behind that, though, the carbureted V-8 has a single muffler with dual tailpipes. The TBI engine gets twin resonators behind the converter, with dual pipes but no muffler.

Points out Leo Szady: "On the TBI Z-28, we've got these two exhaust resonators with twin exhausts. We wanted to get the lowest possible back pressure, and we wanted that nice gurgling sound. But it all had to be below the government's noise-level limits. Both the Z-28 and the Firebird T/A were right up to that 80 db limit that the law allows. We can't exceed that. In fact, we try never to go over 78 db, because we leave a margin for variations from system to system."

Berlinetta's standard engine is the 2.8-liter V-6, borrowed from the J-Car and converted for rwd in S-Trucks. It weighs 73 pounds less than 1981's 3.8 V-6, yet puts out only eight fewer horses—delivers 102 bhp at 5100 rpm.

different intake manifold that didn't have to be designed with an eye to tunnel-wall wet-down—an emissions consideration.

Most engineers concede that, for the moment at least, it would be simpler and more cost effective to modify the carbureted 305 or simply to go to a bigger version of the small-block Chevy V-8—say the 350 or the 400, either of which would drop right in. More than likely, Yenko, Bill Mitchell, and others will have field days offering special high-performance versions of third-generation Camaros.

Al Rasegan, who worked with Russ Gee in developing the Z-28's TBI system and other engine refinements, mentions that there was a lot of early discussion about what engines the Camaro should use in the 1980's. "We talked about whether the car could tolerate a relatively large V-8 or whether it had to be strictly an economy power-

Acceleration Times
Zero to 60 mph, sec.
1982 Camaros

	Manual Trans	Automatic Trans
2.5-liter (151-cid) Four, TBI	15.0	15.0
2.8-liter (173-cid) V-6, 2-bbl.	12.5	14.5
5.0-liter (305-cid) V-8, 4-bbl.	9.5	10.5
5.0-liter (305-cid) V-8, TBI	8.5	9.0

Source: General Motors. All times rounded off to nearest half second.

V-6's starter, alternator, power-steering pump, thermostat housing, and EGR valve had to be repositioned so engine could fit longitudinally in Camaro.

Chevy's 60° V-6 is one of the few remaining GM engines that uses a separate distributor and coil. Narrower vee angle is evident in this photograph.

The carbureted 305 is a carryover engine—RPO LG4/LG3—used in Camaros since 1976. Except for modifications to engine mounts, re-routing wires and hoses, plus lowering the aircleaner, very little had to be changed to adapt this powerplant to the third-generation F-Car.

The V-6, though, is not a carryover. True, Camaros did offer a pair of 3.8-liter, 90-degree V-6's for 1981, but those weren't at all related to this current 60-degree 2.8 liter V-6. General Motors introduced the 2.8 V-6 in its 1980 X-Cars as a transverse engine. Late in 1981, this same engine became available optionally in the rwd Chevy S-10 and GMC S-15 small pickups.

The V-6 took a little more modification than the V-8 to fit into the Camaro's engine compartment. In bringing it around from the X-Car's crosswise to the F-Car's lengthwise positioning, Larry Weathers notes that, "...we had to change the engine-mount locations because the Camaro has a 3-point mount. The intake manifold had to be changed, too, to bring the water outlet up front. On the X-Car's transverse version, the water outlet is toward the flywheel end of the engine, with the EGR [exhaust gas recirculation] valve at the front. In the F-Car, we had to reverse these. We put the EGR toward the rear, the water outlet up front, and we had the usual aircleaner revisions, too."

Additional modifications to adapt the X-Car V-6 to the F-Car included moving the starter and alternator from the engine's left- to its right-hand side, reversing the power-steering pump from right to left, and redesigning the V-6's accessory belt drive to accommodate these repositionings. New pulleys up front also let the V-6 take on a belt-driven fan instead of the X-Car's electric fan.

Since the X-Car's Varajet 2-barrel carburetor tended to flood out on hard turns due to fuel sloshing toward the main metering jet and the accelerator pump, Rochester had to add float-bowl baffles or "stuffers" to the Camaro's version. And, as in the S-Trucks, the large HEI (high energy ignition) distributor gave way to a smaller unit with a separate coil. Finally, because the X-Car's oil filter would have interfered with

The V-6 uses Rochester's 2-barrel Varajet carburetor. It's essentially the J-Car unit, but with baffles added to float bowl to prevent flooding on turns.

Pontiac-built Iron Duke serves as Camaro's base powerplant. It's been a-round for several years, but never with single-point TBI in place of carb.

Replacing the carburetor with the TBI helped get rid of an impressive amount of anti-pollution equipment, notably an expensive smog pump and plumbing.

Not only does base Four give the Camaro nearly 50/50 weight distribution but there's also plenty of underhood space to work on engine and accessories.

the F-Car's engine cradle, a new filter mounting pad had to be designed to tilt the spin-on cannister rearward in the Camaro.

The advantage of the new V-6 over the older ones is obvious. It's a full liter smaller in displacement (2.8 versus 3.8) and weighs 73 pounds less, yet it delivers nearly the same horsepower—102 at 5100 rpm instead of 110. In terms of torque, the new 2.8 V-6 rates 142 lb.ft. at 2400 rpm as against the 3.8s' 170-190 lb.ft. at 2000-1600 rpm.

In the Citation X-11 version, this same new 2.8-liter V-6 delivers 135 bhp at 5400 rpm. The X-11 engine wasn't available for Camaros at the beginning of the 1982 model run, but several sources indicated to me that Chevrolet hoped to include it—or something like the X-11—among forthcoming optional offerings in the Camaro.

Pontiac introduced the 4-cylinder Iron Duke in 1977, concurrently with the division's 301 V-8. These two engines shared the 3.0 x 4.0-inch bore and stroke plus many internal parts. Engineer John Sawruk headed the Iron Duke's mid-1970's development program, and when the engine bowed, it used a Holley/Weber 2-barrel carburetor.

Today, the Iron Duke carries a single-point TBI, controlled by one ECM injector output. You might reasonably expect that this 151-cid Four, with nearly exactly half the 305 V-8's displacement, would use half the V-8's TBI system, namely one 1 13/16-inch throttle bore and half of the 305's ECM. Not so. The two engines' TBI's don't interchange yet, nor do the ECM's. The Four uses a 1 11/16-inch throttle bore and, as noted, it maintains a 12.4-psi fuel pressure instead of the V-8's 10 psi.

The machining line at Rochester Products Div. that manufactures and assembles TBI's does so for all TBI engines, and the designs, of course, are very similar.

Another similarity worth noting is that all three third-generation Camaro engines have identical bore spacing: 4.4 inches. That figure has become something of a Chevrolet hallmark. It harks back to the days of the first small-block Chevy V-8 of

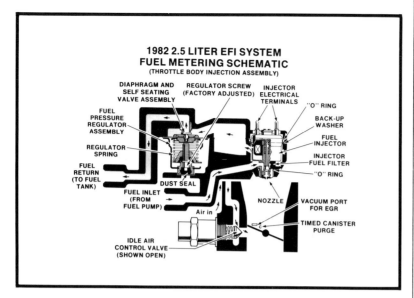

1982 2.5 LITER EFI SYSTEM
FUEL METERING SCHEMATIC
(THROTTLE BODY INJECTION ASSEMBLY)

Iron Duke single-point TBI uses essentially same ECM as twin, but with one computer output instead of two. All GM TBI's are machined on same lines.

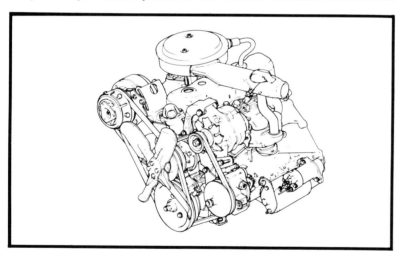

1955. The reason the Pontiac-supplied Iron Duke shares this bore spacing is because it, too, began life as a Chevrolet product (in the Chevy II).

The Four's greatest virtue, certainly, is its extreme thrift. Pre-production checks by General Motors came back with fuel-economy figures of 23 mpg city and 33 mpg highway for the lightest Sport Coupe with the Iron Duke and 4-speed gearbox. Yet this same engine/transmission combination can accelerate the car from zero to 60 mph in just under 15.0 seconds—on a par with many economy imports and a lot more fun to drive.

To sum up, then: The third-generation Camaro still offers a wide range of engines. This wealth of choice makes the marque more appealing to a larger number of owners. And in the years to come, Chevrolet will likely add even greater engine versatility in the form of optional powertrains. □

1982 Camaro
Powertrain Specifications

ENGINES	LQ9	LC1	LG4	LU5
Engine type	In-line 4	60°V-6	90°V-8	90°V-8
Displacement, cu. in.	151	173	305	305
Displacement, cc	2474	2835	4998	4998
Bore, in./mm	4.0/101.6	3.5/89.0	3.74/94.92	3.74/94.92
Stroke, in./mm	3.0/76.2	2.99/76.0	3.48/88.39	3.48/88.39
Bore spacing, in./mm		4.4/111.8		
Compression ratio	8.2:1	8.5:1	8.6:1	9.5:1
Horsepower @ rpm	90 @4000	102 @ 5100	140 @ 4000	165 @ 4200
Torque @ rpm	132 @ 2800	142 @ 2400	240 @ 1600	240 @ 2400
Engine weight, lb.	320.3	371.0	592.5	593.0

INDUCTION SYSTEM				
Type	TBI	Varajet	Quadrajet	TBI
Manufacturer		GM/Rochester Div.		
Number of barrels	1	2	4	2
Barrel diameter, in.	1 11/16	1 3/8 x 1 3/4	1 3/8 x 2 1/4	1 13/16
Flow, cu. ft./min.	325	262	750	650
Choke type	None	Electric	Electric	None
Fuel pump pressure, psi	12.4	6.0-7.5	7.5-9.0	10.0
Fuel tank capacity, gal.		15.54		

EXHAUST SYSTEM				
Type	Single	Single	Single w/2 tailpipes	Dual w/1 exh. pipe
Exhaust manifold		Cast iron		
Exhaust pipe	Stainless	Double-walled stainless steel		
Intermediate pipe	Aluminized steel			Stainless
Number of mufflers	One	One	One	None
Number of resonators	None	None	2 w/Z-28	Two
Tailpipes	Stainless	Aluminized steel		Steel

PISTONS				
Piston material		Aluminum		
Piston weight, oz.	22.96	16.47	17.70	17.70

CRANKSHAFT				
Material		Nodular cast iron		
Number of main brngs.	Five	Four	Five	Five
Main brng. diam., in.	2.300	2.494	2.449	2.449
Bolts per main cap		Two		
Crankpin jrnl. diam., in.	2.000	1.998	2.099	2.099

CONNECTING RODS				
Rod length, in.	6.050	5.700	5.700	5.700
Rod weight, oz.	21.90	21.23	21.23	21.23

CAMSHAFT

Cam drive	Gear	Chain	Chain	Chain
Number of cam brngs.	Three	Four	Five	Five

VALVETRAIN

Valve actuation	———————— Pushrods & rockers ————————			
Lifters	———————— Hydraulic, zero lash ————————			
Pushrod length, in.	8.933	8.933	7.724	7.724
Valve rotators	None	Exhaust	Exhaust	Exhaust
Rocker ratio	1.75	1.50	1.50	1.50

VALVES, INTAKE

Head diameter, in.	1.720	1.600	1.840	1.840
Overall length, in.	4.557	4.700	4.912	4.912
Seat inserts	None	None	None	None
Seat angle	46°	46°	46°	46°
Face angle	45°	45°	45°	45°
Intake opens	33°	25°	44°	38°
Intake closes	79°	81°	76°	92°
Duration	292°	286°	300°	310°
Overlap	23°	7°	44°	n.a.
Lift, in.	.406	.349	.357	.390

VALVES, EXHAUST

Head diameter, in.	1.500	1.300	1.500	1.500
Overall length, in.	4.489	4.730	4.923	4.923
Seat inserts	None	None	None	None
Seat angle	46°	46°	46°	46°
Face angle	45°	45°	45°	45°
Exhaust opens	74°	69°	78°	88°
Exhaust closes	38°	55°	52°	52°
Duration	292°	304°	310°	320°
Overlap	26°	31°	96°	n.a.
Lift, in.	.406	.393	.390	.410

VALVE SPRINGS

Open length, in.	1.254	1.160	1.250	1.250
Closed length, in.	1.660	1.610	1.700	1.700
Lb., valve closed	78-86	76-84	76-84	76-84
Lb., valve open	172-180	194-206	194-206	194-206

IGNITION SYSTEM

Type	———————— Delco HEI, 12 volt ————————			
Coil	Separate	Integral	Integral	Integral
Spark plugs, make	AC	AC	AC	AC
Spark plugs, model	R44TSX	R43TS	R45TS	R45TS
Plug threads	14mm	14mm x 1.25 SAE ————————		
Spark plug gap	.060	.045	.045	.045

ENGINE LUBRICATION

Oil pump type	———————— Gear ————————
To mains, rods	———————— Pressure ————————
To cam, lifters	———————— Pressure ————————
To pistons, pins	———————— Splash ————————
To cylinder walls	———————— Splash ————————

Gauge psi @ 2000 rpm	37.5	50-65	50-65	50-65
Crankcase capacity, qt.	Three	Four	Four	Four
Oil filter capacity, qt.	One	One	One	One

COOLING SYSTEM

Radiator type	———————— Crossflow ————————			
Coolant capacity, qt.	13.1	12.7	15.1	16.1
Cap pressure	———————— 15 psi ————————			
Coolant recovery	———————— Standard ————————			
Thermostat opens	———————— 195° F. ————————			
Std. core width, in.	———————— 20.8 ————————			
Std. core height, in.	———————— 17.2 ————————			
Standard core thickness, in	———————— .925 ————————			
AC/HD core width, in.	26.3	20.8	26.3	26.3
AC/HD core hgt., in.	———————— 17.2 ————————			
AC/HD core thkns., in.	———————— .925 ————————			
Standard fan	———————— Four blades, non-flex ————————			
Optional fan	7 blades	5 blades	7 blades	7 blades
Fan clutch optional?	Yes	Yes	Yes	Yes
Pump type	———————— Centrifugal, belt driven ————————			

1982 Camaro Drivetrain Specifications

	LQ9	LC1	LG4	LU5

CLUTCH

	LQ9	LC1	LG4	LU5
Type	———————— Single dry disc ————————			
Material, facing	———————— Woven molded asbestos ————————			
Manufacturer	———————— Borg & Beck ————————			
Spring load, lbs.	1360	1230-1480	1200-1600	1200-1600
Disc diameter, in.	9.125	9.685	10.34	10.34
Total effective area, in.^{2}	35.94	45.40	50.79	50.79

TRANSMISSION

	LQ9	LC1	LG4	LU5
4-speed manual	Std.	Std.	Std.	Future option
Ratio: First	3.50	3.50	3.42	2.88
Second	2.48	2.48	2.28	1.91
Third	1.66	1.66	1.45	1.33
Fourth	1.00	1.00	1.00	1.00
Reverse	3.50	3.50	3.51	2.78
3-speed automatic	Opt.	Opt.	Opt.	Std.
Type	3-speed automatic w/torque-converter clutch, lockup in high			
Ratio: Low range	———————— 2.74 ————————			
Intermediate range	———————— 1.57 ————————			
High Range	———————— 1.00 ————————			
Reverse	———————— 2.07 ————————			
Max. stall ratio	2.48	2.48	2.15	2.34
Torque converter diam., in.	9.66	11.75	11.75	11.75
Dry capacity, qt.	9.4	9.4	10.6	10.6
Refill capacity, qt.	3.5	3.5	4.25	4.25
Recommended fluid	———————— Dexron II ————————			

REAR-AXLE RATIOS

	LQ9	LC1	LG4	LU5
With manual 4-speed	3.42	3.23	2.73	3.23
With automatic 3-speed	3.08	3.08	2.73	2.93

Chapter Six

Spotlighting the Three Series
Features, Standard Equipment, Options, Etc.

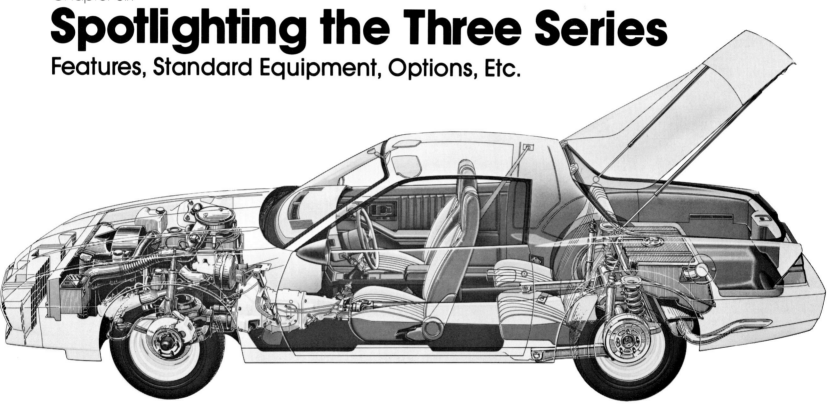

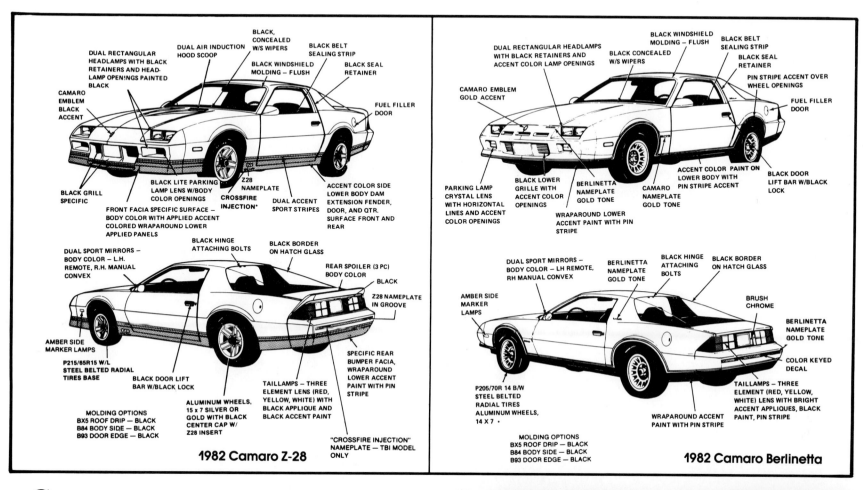

1982 Camaro Z-28

DUAL RECTANGULAR HEADLAMPS WITH BLACK RETAINERS AND HEADLAMP OPENINGS PAINTED BLACK · DUAL AIR INDUCTION HOOD SCOOP · BLACK, CONCEALED W/S WIPERS · BLACK BELT SEALING STRIP · BLACK WINDSHIELD MOLDING — FLUSH · BLACK SEAL RETAINER · FUEL FILLER DOOR · CAMARO EMBLEM BLACK ACCENT · BLACK GRILL SPECIFIC · BLACK LITE PARKING LAMP LENS W/BODY COLOR OPENINGS · Z28 NAMEPLATE · CROSSFIRE INJECTION* · FRONT FACIA SPECIFIC SURFACE — BODY COLOR WITH APPLIED ACCENT COLORED WRAPAROUND LOWER APPLIED PANELS · DUAL ACCENT SPORT STRIPES · ACCENT COLOR SIDE LOWER BODY DAM EXTENSION FENDER, DOOR, AND QTR. SURFACE FRONT AND REAR

DUAL SPORT MIRRORS — BODY COLOR — L.H. REMOTE, R.H. MANUAL CONVEX · BLACK HINGE ATTACHING BOLTS · BLACK BORDER ON HATCH GLASS · REAR SPOILER (3 PC) BODY COLOR · BLACK · Z28 NAMEPLATE IN GROOVE · AMBER SIDE MARKER LAMPS · P215/65R15 W/L STEEL BELTED RADIAL TIRES BASE · BLACK DOOR LIFT BAR W/BLACK LOCK · MOLDING OPTIONS BX5 ROOF DRIP — BLACK, B84 BODY SIDE — BLACK, B93 DOOR EDGE — BLACK · ALUMINUM WHEELS, 15 x 7 SILVER OR GOLD WITH BLACK CENTER CAP W/ Z28 INSERT · TAILLAMPS — THREE ELEMENT LENS (RED, YELLOW, WHITE) WITH BLACK APPLIQUE AND BLACK ACCENT PAINT · "CROSSFIRE INJECTION" NAMEPLATE — TBI MODEL ONLY · SPECIFIC REAR BUMPER FACIA, WRAPAROUND LOWER ACCENT PAINT WITH PIN STRIPE

1982 Camaro Berlinetta

DUAL RECTANGULAR HEADLAMPS WITH BLACK RETAINERS AND ACCENT COLOR LAMP OPENINGS · BLACK WINDSHIELD MOLDING — FLUSH · BLACK CONCEALED W/S WIPERS · BLACK BELT SEALING STRIP · BLACK SEAL RETAINER · PIN STRIPE ACCENT OVER WHEEL OPENINGS · FUEL FILLER DOOR · CAMARO EMBLEM GOLD ACCENT · PARKING LAMP CRYSTAL LENS WITH HORIZONTAL LINES AND ACCENT COLOR OPENINGS · BLACK LOWER GRILLE WITH ACCENT COLOR OPENINGS · BERLINETTA NAMEPLATE GOLD TONE · CAMARO NAMEPLATE GOLD TONE · WRAPAROUND LOWER ACCENT PAINT WITH PIN STRIPE · ACCENT COLOR PAINT ON LOWER BODY WITH PIN STRIPE ACCENT · BLACK DOOR LIFT BAR W/BLACK LOCK

DUAL SPORT MIRRORS — BODY COLOR — LH REMOTE, RH MANUAL CONVEX · BERLINETTA NAMEPLATE GOLD TONE · BLACK HINGE ATTACHING BOLTS · BLACK BORDER ON HATCH GLASS · BRUSH CHROME · BERLINETTA NAMEPLATE GOLD TONE · COLOR KEYED DECAL · AMBER SIDE MARKER LAMPS · P205/70R 14 B/W STEEL BELTED RADIAL TIRES ALUMINUM WHEELS, 14 X 7 · WRAPAROUND ACCENT PAINT WITH PIN STRIPE · TAILLAMPS — THREE ELEMENT (RED, YELLOW, WHITE) LENS WITH BRIGHT ACCENT APPLIQUES, BLACK PAINT, PIN STRIPE · MOLDING OPTIONS BX5 ROOF DRIP — BLACK, B84 BODY SIDE — BLACK, B93 DOOR EDGE — BLACK

CAMAROS AGAIN COME in three distinct series: 1) the performance-oriented Z-28, 2) the luxurious, smooth-riding Berlinetta, and 3) the base Sport Coupe. I'd like to look at each series separately and then examine what they all share jointly.

The All-New Camaro Z-28

Never before has any Z-28 been given so much standard equipment and such a wealth of option choices. Technically, Chevrolet codes the 1982 car 1FP87/Z28, and when you order that series, here's what you get as standard equipment:

All U.S. '82 Z's come standard with the 305 V-8 engine (LG4) with 4-barrel Quadrajet carburetor and dual exhausts. The 4-speed manual wide-ratio transmission (MM4) with 3.42:1 low gear is also standard, as is the special Z-28 handling suspension system.

This suspension includes the 32mm (1.26-inch) front stabilizer bar, the 21mm (0.83-inch) rear stabilizer plus performance calibration of springs, front struts, rear shocks, and high-durometer rubber bushings. The aluminum, 5-spoke, 15x7-inch Z-28 wheels are painted silver or gold and mount Goodyear P215/65R-15 white-letter, steel-belted radial tires.

All Z's come also with the fiberglass SMC (sheet-molded compound) hood, with a special cold-air-induction version for the optional twin throttle-body-injection V-8

Fiberglass "ground effects" rocker extensions grace Z-28. Z's come in eight body colors, with contrasting wraparound stripes above rockers and airdam.

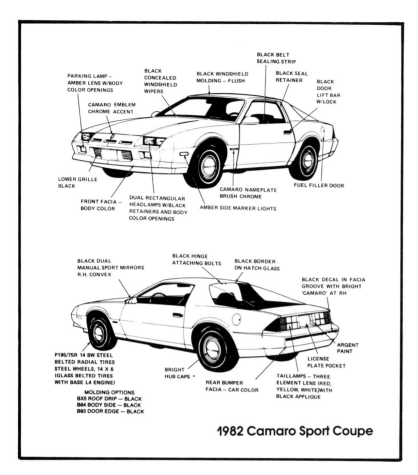

1982 Camaro Sport Coupe

Labels on top illustration:
- PARKING LAMP – AMBER LENS W/BODY COLOR OPENINGS
- BLACK CONCEALED WINDSHIELD WIPERS
- BLACK WINDSHIELD MOLDING – FLUSH
- BLACK BELT SEALING STRIP
- BLACK SEAL RETAINER
- BLACK DOOR LIFT BAR W/LOCK
- CAMARO EMBLEM CHROME ACCENT
- LOWER GRILLE BLACK
- FRONT FACIA – BODY COLOR
- DUAL RECTANGULAR HEADLAMPS W/BLACK RETAINERS AND BODY COLOR OPENINGS
- CAMARO NAMEPLATE BRUSH CHROME
- AMBER SIDE MARKER LIGHTS
- FUEL FILLER DOOR

Labels on bottom illustration:
- BLACK DUAL MANUAL SPORT MIRRORS R.H. CONVEX
- BLACK HINGE ATTACHING BOLTS
- BLACK BORDER ON HATCH GLASS
- BLACK DECAL IN FACIA GROOVE WITH BRIGHT 'CAMARO' AT RH
- P195/75R 14 BW STEEL BELTED RADIAL TIRES STEEL WHEELS, 14 X 6 (GLASS BELTED TIRES WITH BASE L4 ENGINE)
- MOLDING OPTIONS BX5 ROOF DRIP – BLACK B84 BODY SIDE – BLACK B93 DOOR EDGE – BLACK
- BRIGHT HUB CAPS •
- REAR BUMPER FACIA – CAR COLOR
- LICENSE PLATE POCKET
- TAILLAMPS – THREE ELEMENT LENS (RED, YELLOW, WHITE) WITH BLACK APPLIQUE
- ARGENT PAINT

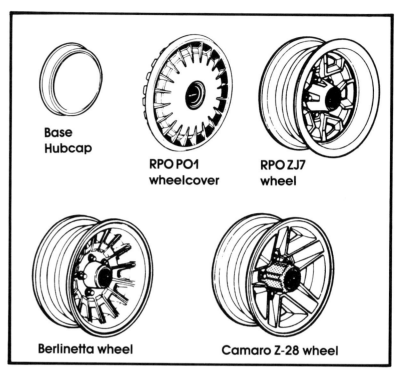

Base Hubcap

RPO PO1 wheelcover

RPO ZJ7 wheel

Berlinetta wheel

Camaro Z-28 wheel

(LU5). Every Z-28 also carries full instrumentation, including tachometer, working gauges, and a quartz analog rally clock in the console.

The base Camaro interior is upgraded in the Z-28 to include carpeted kick panels, and all Z's have the leather-wrapped, round-hub steering wheel plus leather grips for gear-shifters and parking brake. Fast-ratio power steering with the 12.7:1 gear is also part of the package, as are dual body-color sport mirrors and a vanity mirror on the passenger's sunvisor.

Viewing the new Z-28 from the outside, you'll notice a specific front fascia with an integral airdam beneath the bumper, black-lens parking lamps, and "ground-effects" rocker extensions with special accent trim. Around back, all Z's have an integrated, 3-piece, bolt-on decklid spoiler.

Those make up the major standard items for all third-generation Z-28's. In addition—and for the Z-28 only—you can further order the following factory options:

The 305 V-8 with twin throttle-body injectors is coded LU5 and represents the ultimate in Z-28 power and performance. With this engine you get the special SMC hood—the one with twin cold-air intakes or "flappers" that open via an electric solenoid when you floorboard the accelerator. The command to this solenoid comes from the same ECM that controls the TBI (via the throttle-position sensor).

According to Camaro design-studio chief Jerry Palmer, "Tom Zimmer, Fred Schaasfsma, and some of us were out at the Milford Proving Grounds, watching the

Each series gets a specific wheel, with PO1 wheelcover and ZJ7 rim available optionally only on base Camaro. Goodyear supplies Z-28's sticky tires.

Arizona mountie stopped ad agency's 1982 prototype so he could get a closer look. California Highway Patrol has been using Z-28 cruisers for several years.

Camaro's Fisher-built T-top carries a double seal where glass panels meet roof. This new type of seal plus flush fits keep down wind noise.

Berlinetta's 11 body colors receive complementary lower accents in either charcoal, blue, jade, black, or dark gold. Extensive use of gold accents include pinstriping, wheel backgrounds, and emblems. Custom interiors, standard in the Berlinetta, come in 6 colors: black, camel, jade, blue, silver, maroon.

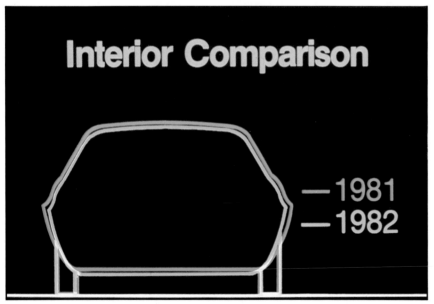

Interior Comparison

— 1981
— 1982

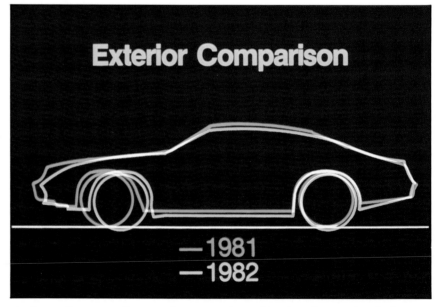

Exterior Comparison

— 1981
— 1982

Camaro's 1981 silhouettes are slightly larger than those of 1982, but new car's weight is down an average of almost 500 pounds while still keeping

similar seating space. Rear overhang was dictated by size of spare tire. Body stands about an inch nearer road, which brings down '82's overall height.

The Z-28 makes an excellent road car. Its responsiveness and precise handling give the driver total control. It's especially cooperative on twisty byways.

Conteur driver's seat (center) and 6-way power buckets stand out among many Camaro interior options. All seats recline, and glovebox lid doubles as armrest.

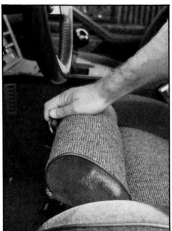

Conteur's grip on driver isn't so fierce as some aftermarket seats, but it holds a person in place. Designers insisted on making all controls easy to reach.

With console now standard in every Camaro, this area gets more visual and practical emphasis than ever before. Console takes on a number of functions previously reserved for the instrument panel. ERS emblem above heater controls (right) signify extended range speakers.

Nothing has increased the Camaro's carrying capacity so much as making it a hatchback with folding rear seat.

A total of 30.9 cubic feet of cargo can be stuffed into the Camaro's hatch, including six suitcases, two golfbags, three cases, and two soft garment bags.

Recessed well under deck floor has room for another 4.3 cubic feet of cargo, permits groceries to be carried upright. Lid (optional) hides valuable items.

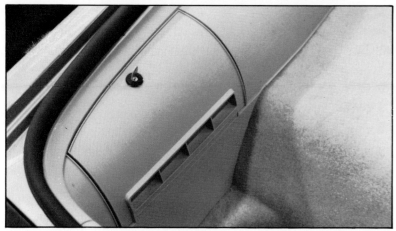

Another storage area rests in left rear quarter, harbors cameras and such. It's vented to prevent heat buildup and lockable with some interior combos.

Z-28 prototypes run. Fred says, 'You know, I have a sneaking suspicion that we're not getting enough air to the twin TBI setup.' So about 10 days later, the engineers had a chance to run some tests and correlate information on the SMC hood with and without the flapper valves. They found that the cold-air intakes are good for just about one second in 0-60-mph acceleration times." That gives the Z a 0-60 time of 8.5 seconds as clocked by Chevrolet at Milford.

The engineers couldn't decide at first whether to make the Z-28 hood from steel, aluminum, or fiberglass. General Tire & Rubber Co. had been fabricating SMC hoods for Corvettes for several years, so Chevy drew on that experience to have General supply similar hoods for the Z-28. Comments F-Car Project Center chief engineer Steve Major, "The SMC hood reduces mass [weight] by about nine kilograms or approximately 20 pounds." And Bob Haglund adds, "You might be interested to know that the Z's SMC hood represents some impressive firsts for Chevrolet. It's the largest of this type we've ever done, dwarfing the X-11's and even the Corvette's. Also, it's installed before painting, so it has to withstand elpo oven temperatures of 375-400° F. Since it has

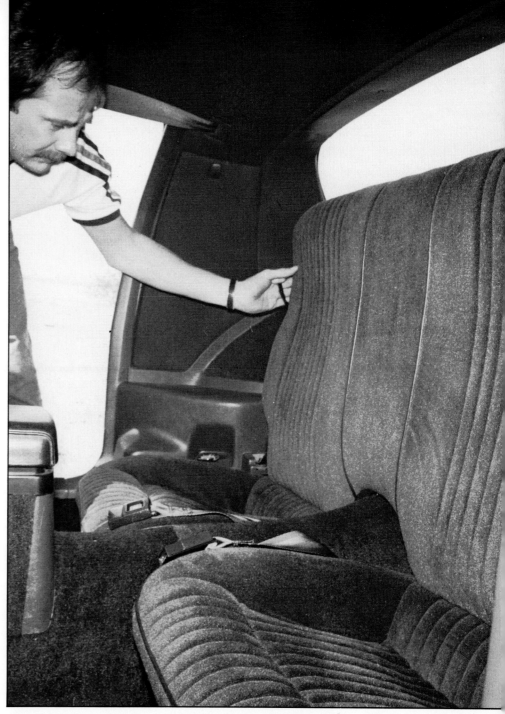

Deeply recessed rear buckets grip riders, increase headroom. Rear seatback folds forward, and this area is accessible either through door or rear hatch.

Perfect for medium-sized impedimenta, storage well holds nearly as much as previous generation's trunk. Electrical connectors for hatch rest at left of *striker. Striker mounts in rubber to damp out boom. Liftover sill stands no higher than '81 Camaro's trunk lip. Seatback can be lowered from rear, too.*

Black parking lamps fit into simulated brake air intakes in Z-28. The inner headlight stands slightly ahead of outboard one. Adjustments are under hood.

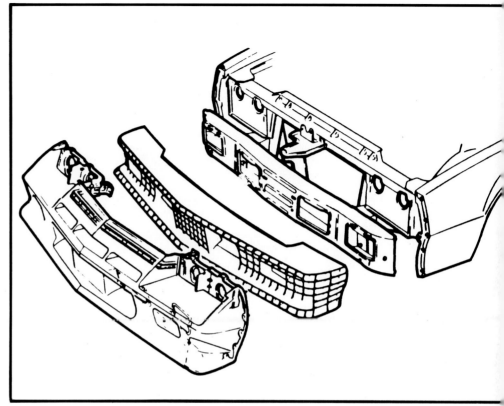

Enersorber front bumper uses same Guideflex honeycomb as rear, can take 5-mph hit without deforming. Impact bar is aluminum or high-strength steel.

to be electrostatically painted along with the steel portions of the body, we've had to work out a special conductive undercoat for the SMC hood—quite a neat trick.''

With the LU5 V-8, you have to take GM's Turbo Hydra-matic 200c automatic transmission (MX1). The automatic supplied with either V-8 has been beefed internally to withstand the additional torque. Chevrolet tells me the close-ratio manual 4-speed (MM4) will become available for the twin TBI V-8 sometime around mid-1982. When it does, that transmission will have the 2.88:1 low gear.

An interesting new option for the Z-28 is RPO J65, the 4-wheel disc brakes. Actually, these brakes are available for any V-8-engined Camaro, not just the Z. You have to order the G80 limited-slip differential at the same time as the 4-wheel discs, and with the G80 comes the stowaway collapsible spare tire.

The Camaro's 4-wheel discs use the standard 10.5-inch vented front rotors plus new 9.5-inch rear rotors. Both sets incorporate low-drag calipers.

Inside the Z-28, and available *only* in this series, is a special driver's seat supplied by Lear-Siegler. It's called the *Conteur* seat (RPO AQ9), and it's fully adjustable for lumbar and thigh support, for backrest angle, and for headrest position. You can also adjust the backrest lateral restraint wings and cushion for comfort. When you order the Conteur, you get an identically trimmed but ordinary Camaro passenger's seat with the

Three-piece urethane spoiler remains standard on Z-28, is available on base Sport Coupe and Berlinetta. Wraparound tail lamps double as side markers.

Camaro's clean, understated lines present themselves from every view. Big rear glass can be electrically heated, and there's a rear wiper option as well.

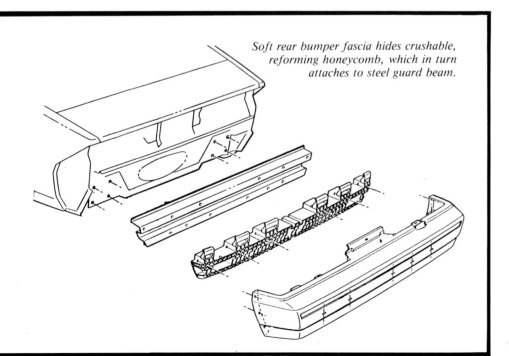

Soft rear bumper fascia hides crushable, reforming honeycomb, which in turn attaches to steel guard beam.

fixed headrest and no specialized adjustments. You *cannot* order two Conteur seats in one car.

In terms of structural differences between the Z-28 and other series, the Z includes a special rail reinforcement at the steering gear, a brace on the right-hand strut tower, braces on the front-suspension crossmember, and added stiffness at the Panhard rod brace. The Panhard-rod bushings are also stiffer than normal, as are all bushings in the Z's front and rear suspension systems.

The New Berlinetta

Nor has Chevrolet rested in its effort to improve and sweeten the Berlinetta. It's still Camaro's grand-touring car, with the same previous virtues of luxury and silence. But it now lists some extra touches that weren't available in the past.

When you order a Model 1FS87 Berlinetta, the 2.8-liter, 2-barrel V-6 engine (LC1) comes standard, as does the 4-speed manual gearbox (MM4) with 3.50:1 low. There's no more 3-speed available for any third-generation Camaro.

Also standard in the Berlinetta, as before, is the Custom interior (B18), which uses up-level upholstery and special trim on the seats and door panels. Another item of standard equipment is RPO BS1, the so-called Quiet Sound Group, which uses additional body insulation under the Custom interior's heavier carpets and extra padding up against the firewall. The Berlinetta further gets a 6mm molded headliner instead of the 3mm foam thickness in the non-Custom interior, and it also includes some acoustical insulation even beyond the BS1 group.

Too, a lockable, hinged cargo floor extension that covers the rear storage well is part of the Berlinetta's Custom interior, as is a lockable rear side stowage compartment and carpeting on the load-deck sidewall area, over the wheelhouses, and on the rear inner panel.

The Berlinetta gets the same right-hand visor vanity mirror, outside mirrors, and fully instrumented gauge cluster as the Z-28, including the tach and console-mounted quartz rally clock.

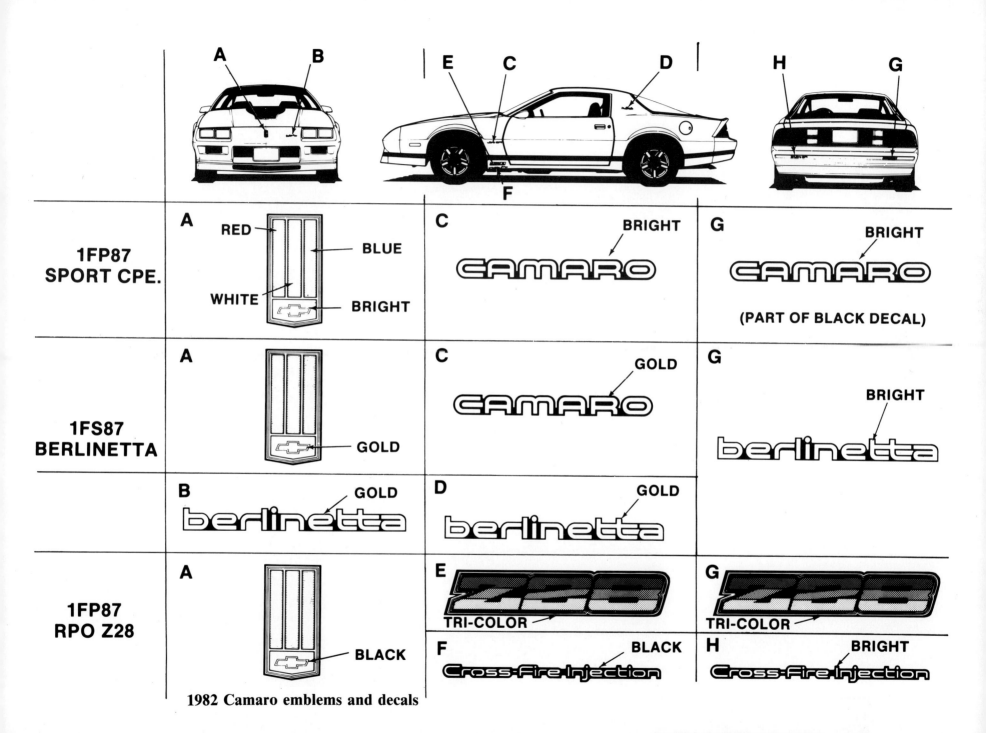

	A	C	G
1FP87 SPORT CPE.	A — RED, BLUE, WHITE, BRIGHT	C — BRIGHT — **CAMARO**	G — BRIGHT — **CAMARO** (PART OF BLACK DECAL)
1FS87 BERLINETTA	A — GOLD	C — GOLD — **CAMARO**	G — BRIGHT — *berlinetta*
	B — GOLD — *berlinetta*	D — GOLD — *berlinetta*	
1FP87 RPO Z28	A — BLACK	E — TRI-COLOR — **Z28**	G — TRI-COLOR — **Z28**
	1982 Camaro emblems and decals	F — BLACK — *Cross-Fire-Injection*	H — BRIGHT — *Cross-Fire-Injection*

FLUSH WINDSHIELD DESIGN

OLD DESIGN

**OFFSET GLASS WITH EXTRUDED
ALUMINUM REVEAL MOLDING.**

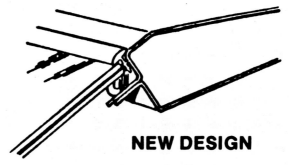

NEW DESIGN

**FLUSH GLASS WITH EXTRUDED
PLASTIC MOLDING**

Camaros have no bright trim. Black moldings often serve a double function in decorating and sealing at same time. Simplified windshield molding puts glass nearer metal surface, again helps smooth airflow for less wind noise and slightly better aerodynamics. Extruded moldings also aid glass installers.

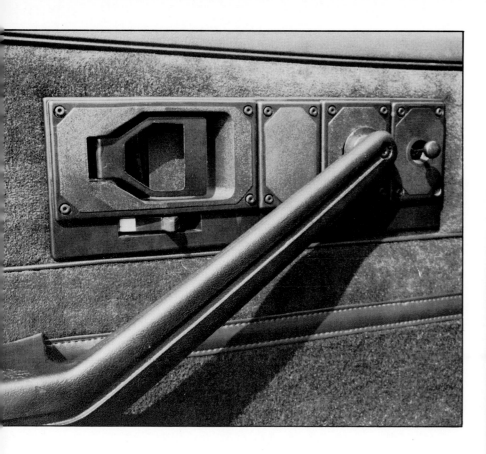

The Berlinetta's suspension system is calibrated for a much smoother, gentler ride than the Z. It comes with softer bushings, strut mounts, and front/rear spring isolators. The Berlinetta also gets specific strut and shock valving plus rear shock-absorber isolators that are larger than those found on the base Sport Coupe. Specific aluminum 14x7-inch wheels with gold-painted backgrounds are the only factory rims you can get for the Berlinetta. These mount low-rolling-resistance, steel-belted, P205/70R-14 blackwall tires.

The gold background in the wheels complements the gold that's included in every combination of the Berlinetta's pinstriping. Berlinettas for 1982 are available in 11 solid body colors—the most for any series Camaro—with pinstripes in combinations of gold plus either charcoal, black, dark blue, dark gold, or dark jade.

Options for the Berlinetta are basically the same as for the Z-28, but you can't get the Z's Conteur seat nor the twin TBI V-8. You *can* get the 6-way power seat (AG9) in the Berlinetta or for any other new Camaro. The only optional tires for the Berlinetta are a full set of steel-belted pinstripe whitewalls. For a detailed option list, see page 93.

The Basic Sport Coupe

You can order the Camaro base Sport Coupe (Model 1FP87) either with or without optional goodies. But even in its most austere form, you still get an amazing array of standard items.

For example, every new Camaro comes with power front disc brakes. When you

Gas struts support hood as well as rear hatch. Hidden wipers contain fluidic washers that move with arms. Hood swings forward for wiper-blade access.

Gracefully sculpted "semi-patch" mirrors replace lollipop types used before. Side-glass de-icers in upper corners of i.p. deck keep windows from fogging up.

specify certain engine and air-conditioner combinations*, the finned rear drums are aluminum-backed for better cooling and reduced weight.

You also get power steering as standard equipment, with a 15.0:1 gear ratio for the base Sport Coupe, 14.0:1 for the F41 handling package, variable-ratio 15/13:1 for the Berlinetta and, as mentioned, 12.7:1 in the Z-28. The 4-cylinder base car uses an Acme worm-and-roller steering gear, while all other Camaros have the recirculating-ball type.

Inside the base Camaro, the standard instrument cluster has warning lights instead of gauges for temperature, oil pressure, and alternator. There's the same double-pointer speedometer as in the Z-28 and Berlinetta, though, plus the same million-mile odometer. This odometer registers from 000,000 to 999,999 and then rolls back to zero the second time around.

*The Four without air, the V-6 automatic with air (Sport Coupe only), TBI V-8 4-speed with air, or the TBI V-8 automatic without air. All other combinations use finned cast-iron rear drums.

Also standard, as in years past, are bucket seats and central floor console. Buckets for the Sport Coupe come in all six Camaro interior colors, and they're available either in full vinyl or in a combination of vinyl and cloth. All front buckets recline and have inertia seatback latches. Standard consoles are black and have a built-in glovebox plus separate ashtrays for front and rear passengers.

A heater with forced air to side-window defoggers is likewise standard, as are all the following: a day/night rearview mirror, cigarette lighter, inside hood release, door armrests with integral pull handles, provisions for two front speakers and two rear speakers, color-keyed carpeting on the front and rear floors, carpeting on the cargo floor and down inside the rear storage well, and a carpeted folding rear seatback that extends the cargo deck length to just over five feet (61.3 inches).

As for optional equipment, you can order the Custom interior (RPO B18) for both the base Camaro Sport Coupe and the Z-28. With it you get complete upgrading to the level of the Berlinetta, including full acoustical insulation, carpeting on kick panels

FUEL TANK AND SPARE TIRE PLACEMENT

Fuel tank tucks neatly out of harm's way between rear seat and storage well. It's protected here, and the tank's wedge shape gives plenty of axle clearance.

and console sidewalls, and up-level door panels with carpeted lower sections. Another interior option, B48, provides deluxe baggage compartment trim for the Sport Coupe and Z-28. Included in B48 are carpeted rear side trim, carpeting inside the storage well, and a locking rear side stowage compartment.

And you can replace the Sport Coupe's base 2.5-liter TBI Four with any Camaro engine except the twin-TBI V-8. The V-6 or the carbureted V-8 (LC1 or LG4) upgrade the Sport Coupe's performance, while the F41 suspension package gives it handling that approaches the Z-28.

The Camaro's optional air conditioner (C60) is the semi-modular type. The evaporator loads through the firewall from inside the car, as does the heater core.

Then, too, there's an entirely new combination of factory sound equipment for third-generation Camaros: Delco's 2000 series. All radios—including the basic AM—come with at least dual 4x6-inch coaxial front speakers mounted just below the windshield ahead of the driver and passenger. All stereo AM/FM radios add a pair of extended-range, 6x9-inch, dual-cone speakers mounted in the rear side panels.

Round fuel-filler door, made of high-impact plastic, seals against a plastic inner liner. Non-corroding fuel door can be ordered with an optional lock.

Chevrolet's early plans called for two actual Indy 500 pace cars to be built, both fully loaded 1982 Z-28's with the '83 Camaro's Custom interior, twin- *TBI V-8, and T-top. Each dealer would get one replica to sell. All 5500 replicas reflected the originals' blue-on-silver paint scheme and Indy graphics.*

There's a choice of five sound systems in all: the AM radio (U63), AM/FM (U69), AM/FM stereo (YEI), AM/FM stereo with cassette player (YE3), and AM/FM with 8-track stereo (YE4). The last three come with extended-range rear speakers (denoted by a small ''ERS'' tag on the instrument panel), and the two tape-playing radios (YE3 and YE4) come with integral digital clocks. ERS front coaxial speakers use larger cones, and the rear ones have more powerful magnets than non-ERS sound systems.

The digital clocks take precedent over the console-mounted rally clock that's ordinarily standard in Berlinettas and Z-28's. This means that if you order the YE3 or YE4 sound systems in those series, you end up *without* the console-mounted rally clock; just the digital clock in the radio. And you *can* get the digital clock optionally with any of the non-tape-playing radios.

Controls for the optional power windows, rear hatch release, and power outside mirrors all rest on the console. So does the parking-brake lever—the first time it's ever been mounted there in a Camaro. In all previous models, the parking brake was set with the driver's left foot. This made it pretty tough for the driver to use in conjunction with the clutch pedal—as in starting from an uphill stop sign.

CAMARO

Another stable of Camaro pace cars has been set up by PPG Industries, which sponsors 10 races each season in the CART world series. PPG's Camaros take styling inspiration from IMSA Kelly American Challenge cars. Early in the '82 season, PPG considered modifying its Camaros with Corvette 350 TBI turbos.

Another interesting option is the Fisher-supplied hatch roof. The glass panels are removable individually and have dual lip seals to prevent leakage and wind noise. The panels store in protective vinyl bags that strap to the cargo-deck floor.

In all, Chevrolet has made this third-generation Camaro the height not only of fashion but of comfort, performance, luxury, and personalization. You can tailor any Camaro just about any way you want. And I understand that this is a trend that'll continue into the future.

There's already talk, even at this early stage, of equipping Camaros with 5-speed manual transmissions and split 50/50 rear seatbacks for more versatile loading. As production and assembly facilities for the Z-28's Conteur seat increase, look for greater availability of that option, too.

Even now, though, as in the past, the third-generation Camaro sets the standard for all the world's ponycars. It remains unique and as much a leader as ever. Its leadership seems to increase as the car matures. Other ponycars copy the Camaro—never the other way around. And an auto that gains in status and stature as it grows older remains a solid bargain everywhere along the line—buying, selling, or driving. □

1982 Camaro Body Specifications

External Body Dimensions, inches

Wheelbase 101.0
Overall length 187.8
Overall height 49.8
Overall width 70.6
Width with doors open 155.1
Overhang, front/rear 42.5/44.3
Tread, front/rear 60.7/61.6
Minimum ground clearance 4.8
Point of min. grd. clearance . Front crossmember

Internal Body Dimensions, inches

Head room, front/rear 37.0/35.6
Leg room, front/rear 43.0/28.6
Shoulder room, front/rear 57.5/56.3
Hip room, front/rear 56.3/42.8
Steering-wheel angle . . . . .18°
Front seatback angle . . . . 26.5°
Front seat travel 7.56

Luggage Compartment Dimensions

Capacity, seatback up, cu. ft. 11.6
Capacity, seatback down, cu. ft. 30.9
Trunk lift-over height, in. 15.0
"Well" dimensions, in. . . . . 14x13x41.
Cargo deck, max. length, in. 61.3
Cargo deck, max. width, in. . . . . .56.0.

Glass Dimensions

Windshield slope angle . . . . 62°
Backlight slope angle . . . . .71°
Windshield glass, type . . . . . Curved, laminated
Side & rear glass, type . . . . Curved, tempered
Windshield exposed area, in.^{2} 1395.1
Side glass exposed area, in.^{2} 1010.6
Backlight exposed area, in.^{2} 966.0
Total exposed glass surface, in.^{2} 3371.7

SPORTY 2 + 2 INTERIOR SIZE
OVER/UNDER 1981 CAMARO
(INCHES)

	FRONT	REAR
HEAD ROOM	37.0 (+0.1)	35.6 (−0.1)
LEG ROOM	43.0 (−0.9)	28.6 (+0.2)
SHOULDER ROOM	57.5 (+0.1)	56.3 (+1.9)
HIP ROOM	56.3 (+1.0)	42.8 (−3.5)

1982 Camaro Chassis Specifications

Steering

Type . . . . .Saginaw power steering, parallelogram linkage. Acme worm type in base Sport Coupe, recirculating ball in all others.

Steering gear ratios
Sport Coupe . . . . 15.0:1.
Berlinetta (variable) . . . . 15.0/13.0:1.
F41 option . . . . 14.0:1.
Z-28 . . . . 12.7:1.

Overall steering ratio
Sport Coupe . . . . 15.3:1.
Berlinetta (variable) . . . . 15.3/13.3:1.
F41 option . . . . 14.3:1.
Z-28 . . . . 13.0:1.

Wheel turns, lock to lock
Sport Coupe . . . . 2.9.
Berlinetta . . . . 2.7.
F41 option . . . . 3.0.
Z-28 . . . . 2.5.

Steering valve effort, in.-lb.
Sport Coupe . . . . 17-23.
Berlinetta . . . . 17-23.
F41 option . . . . 24-30.
Z-28 . . . . 24-30.

Pump orifice flow rate, gal./min.
2.5-liter Four . . . . 1.7-2.1.
2.8-liter V-6 . . . . 2.4-2.8.
5.0-liter V-8 . . . . 3.1-3.5.

Curb turn diam., ft. . . . . 36.7.
Rag joint . . . . 4-ply (Z-28, 7-ply).

Suspension, front

Type . . . . .Modified MacPherson struts with coil springs between crossmember and lower A-arms; front stabilizer bar standard in all models. Kahr-Lon low-friction lower balljoint. Ball-bearing upper strut mount on all but base Sport Coupe.

Alignment, curb
Caster . . . . Plus 3.0 degr.
Camber . . . . Plus 1.0 degr.
Toe-in . . . . Plus 0.4 degr.
(Z-28 is plus 0.3 degr).

Stabilizer bar diam., in.
Sport Coupe & Berlinetta . . . . 1.064 (27mm).
F41 option . . . . 1.182 (30mm).
Z-28 . . . . 1.261 (32mm).

Spring rates, lb./in.
Sport Coupe & Berlinetta . . . . 330.
F41 option . . . . 365.
Z-28 . . . . 550.

LCA bushing, front, lb./in. 50,000
(Z-28, 75,000).
LCA bushing, rear, lb./in. 17,000
(Z-28, 30,000).
Strut-mount rate, lateral, lb./in. 8,600
(Z-28, 17,000).
Full jounce/rebound, in. . . . . 2.96/3.74.

Suspension, rear

Type . . . . Torque arm secured to live rear axle housing and transmission mount. Coil springs and tubular hydraulic shock absorbers on lower trailing arms. Lateral, diagonal track bar. Rear stabilizer bar on all but Sport Coupe and Berlinetta.

Stabilizer bar diam., in.
F41 . . . . .0.709 (18mm).
Z-28 . . . . .0.827 (21mm).

Spring rates, lb./in.
All but Z-28 . . . . 100.
Z-28 . . . . 180.

Full jounce/rebound, in. . . . . 3.3/4.6.

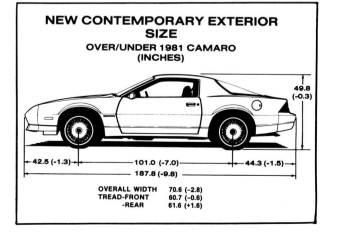

NEW CONTEMPORARY EXTERIOR SIZE
OVER/UNDER 1981 CAMARO
(INCHES)

49.8 (−0.3)

42.5 (−1.3)   101.0 (−7.0)   44.3 (−1.5)
187.8 (−9.8)

OVERALL WIDTH	70.6 (−2.8)
TREAD-FRONT	60.7 (−0.6)
-REAR	61.6 (+1.6)

Wheels & Tires

Sport Coupe . . . . Pressed and welded steel, 14x6, 0.5-in. offset; P195/75-R14 low-rolling-resistance, steel-belted radial bw tires (glass-belted w/4cyl. engine).

Berlinetta . . . . Cast aluminum alloy wheels, 15 spokes, gold-painted backgrounds, 14x7, 0.34-in. offset; P205/70-R14 low-rolling-resistance, bw, steel-belted radial tires.

Z-28 . . . . Cast aluminum alloy wheels, 5 spokes, painted, 15x7, 0.30-in. offset; P215/65-R15 steel-belted radial bw tires.

Tire pressures, f/r, psi . . . . 35/35.
Number of lug studs . . . . 5.
Lug circle diameter, in. . . . . 4.75.
Std. spare wheel size, in. . . . . 15x4.
Std. spare tire size . . . . T125/70-D15 (P195/75-D14 w/Positraction).

Brakes

Type . . . . 4-wheel hydraulic, vented discs front, duo-servo drums rear; vacuum booster std.; self-adjusting.

Front rotor diam., in. . . . . 10.5.
Front rotor thickness, in. . . . . 1.03.
Rear drum diam., in. . . . . 9.5.
Rear drum material . . . . Finned cast iron. Aluminum used in some applications (see text).
Opt. rear rotor diam., in. . . . . 9.5.
Opt. rear rotor thickness, in. . . . . 0.83.
Disc pad lining material . . . . . Semi-metallic.
Caliper assembly . . . . Vented, 2.5-in. piston.
Drum shoe material . . . . Asbestos.
Master cylinder . . . . . . Aluminum body, plastic see-thru reservoir, tandem vacuum booster.
Master cylinder, bore/stroke,in.. . . . . 0.94 x 1.46 (w/4-wheel discs, 1.00 x 1.47).
Front/rear piston diam., in. . 2.5/0.75 (std. brakes).
Power booster . . . . Vacuum, 7.87 x 7.87 in.; 4-cyl. engine comes with vacuum pump.
Effective braking area, sq. in. . . . . 95.42.
Total lining area, sq. in. . . . . 107.22.
Total swept area, sq. in. . . . . 307.7.

Major RPO Option Index
1982 Camaro

RPO code	Item	base Sport Coupe	Berli-netta	Z-28
AG9	6-way power seat	O	O	O
AQ9	Contour driver's seat	na	na	O
AU3	Power door locks	O	O	O
AO1	Tinted glass	O	O	O
A31	Power windows	O	O	O
A90	Power remote hatch release	O	O	O
BS1	Quiet Sound Group	O	S	O
BX5	Roof-rail drip moldings (na with CCI)	O	O	O
B18	Custom interior	O	S	O
B32	Front floormats, color-keyed	O	O	O
B33	Rear floormats, color-keyed	O	O	O
B48	Deluxe cargo-area trim (req. Custom interior)	O	S	O
B84	Body side moldings	O	O	O
B93	Door edge guard moldings	O	O	O
CC1	Hatch roof with removable glass panels	O	O	O
CD4	Intermittent windshield wipers	O	O	O
C25	Rear wiper and washer for glass hatch	O	O	O
C49	Rear window defogger, electric	O	O	O
C60	Air conditioner	O	O	O
DG7	Electrically adjustable outside mirrors (2)	O	O	O
D35	Sport outside mirrors, LH remote (2)	O	S	S
D60	Special-order paint colors	O	O	O
D80	Rear decklid spoiler	O	O	S
F41	Handling suspension (req. ZJ7 & QYC)	O	na	na
G80	Limited-slip differential (incl. Stowaway spare tire)	O	O	O
J65	4-Wheel disc brakes, power (req. V-8 & G80)	O	O	O
K35	Speed control w/resume speed	O	O	O
LQ9	Engine, 2.5 litre 4 w/TBI	S	na	na
LC1	Engine, 2.8 liter V-6	O	S	na
LG4	Engine, 5.0 liter V-8	O	O	S
LU5	Engine, 5.0 liter V-8 w/TBI	na	na	O
MM4	Transmission, 4-speed manual	S	S	S
MX1	Transmission, Turbo Hydra-matic 200C	O	O	O
NA5	Emission-control equipment	S	S	S
N33	Comfortilt adjustable steering column	O	O	O

RPO code	Item	base Sport Coupe	Berli-netta	Z-28
PO1	Wheelcovers	O	na	Na
QVJ	Tires, P195/75R-14 steel radials, whitewall	O	na	na
QXV	Tires, P195/75R-14 steel radials, blackwall	O	na	na
QYC	Tires, P205/70R-14 steel radials, white lettered (req. ZJ7)	O	na	na
QYF	Tires, P195/75R-14 glass radials, blackwall	S	na	na
QYA	Tires, 205/70R-14 steel-belted radials, black	na	S	na
QYG	Tires, 195/75R-14 steel radials, white stripe	O	na	na
QYH	Tires, 215/65R-15 steel-belted radials, white letter	na	na	S
QVU	Tires, 205/70R-14 steel radials, white stripe	na	O	na
TR9	Auxiliary light group	O	O	O
TT5	Halogen high-beam headlamps	O	O	O
UA1	Heavy-duty battery	O	O	O
UE8	Digital clock (incl. w/YE3 & YE4)	O	O	O
UO5	Dual horns	O	S	O
U21	Instrumentation with full gauges and tachometer	O	S	S
U35	Electric console clock, quartz	O	S	S
U63	Radio, AM w/dual front speakers	O	O	O
U69	Radio, AM/FM with dual front speakers	O	O	O
U73	Antenna (incl. with all radios)	O	O	O
U75	Antenna, electric (req. U63, U69, YE1, YE3, YE4 radios)	O	O	O
U81	Speakers, dual rear (req. U63 or U69)	O	O	O
VO8	Heavy-duty cooling system	O	O	O
YE1	Radio, AM/FM stereo, ext. range, 4 speakers	O	O	O
YE3	Radio, AM/FM stereo w/cassette player	O	O	O
YE4	Radio, AM/FM stereo with 8-track, ext. range (incl. UE8)	O	O	O
YF5	Emission-control equipment for California only	O	O	O
ZJ7	Steel Rally wheels, color-keyed	O	na	na

Symbols: O = optional, S = standard, na = not available.

THE GREAT
CAMARO

Michael Lamm's fantastic Camaro book covers all years from 1967 through 1981. It's the original marque history, published initially in 1978 and updated several times since. Chocked full of photos – both black and white and color – this hardcover book includes complete engineering and styling details, interviews, specifications, production figures, options, and listings of year-to-year changes. Chapters highlight the Z-28, Camaro's racing triumphs, etc. It's *the* definitive Camaro book! **The Camaro Book from A to Z-28.**

Hardcover; plastic-laminated dust-jacket. **Size:** 8½ x 11 inches, 144 pages, horizontal format. **Photos:** 187, with 16 pages in full color. Coated stock throughout. ISBN 0-932128-00-9.

Suggested retail price . . . U.S. $16.95

Here's the most complete, most detailed book ever published for Firebird and Trans Am enthusiasts. Author/publisher Michael Lamm details all 1967-81 models, with full engineering and design histories. Interviews with the important people involved in developing Firebirds. High-performance and racing particulars. Options, accessories, and year-to-year changes. Information on the 1973-74 Super Duty 455 engine, Special- and Limited-Edition models, the Tenth Anniversary Trans Am, and the Turbo T/A. Suspension specifics, and much, much more. You won't find a wider range of photos, information, and specifications anywhere!

Hardcover; plastic-laminated dust-jacket. **Size:** 8½ x 11 inches, 160 pages, horizontal format. **Photos:** 321, with 16 pages in full color. Coated stock throughout. ISBN 0-932128-01-7.

Suggested retail price . . .U.S. $18.95.

Chevrolet's all-new 1982 Camaro – the first major model change in 12 years – brings recharged excitement to American motoring. Michael Lamm's book captures the new generation's verve and goes into great detail on this Camaro's engineering and design conception, its many changed features, its exceptional personality and performance. The book takes lengthy looks at such specifics as the Z-28's dual throttle-body fuel injection, its fully adjustable Conteur driver's seat, its 4-wheel disc brakes, and all its many engineering nuances. Much attention, too, is lavished on the new Berlinetta and Sport Coupe. Again, interviews lend depth, and photos abound!

Hardcover; plastic-laminated dust-jacket. **Size;** 8½ x 11 inches, 96 pages, horizontal format. **Photos:** 209, with 16 pages in full color. Coated stock throughout. ISBN 0-932128-02-5.

Suggested retail price . . .U.S. $14.95

Alphabetical Index

Acknowledgements

Daniel T. Agresta, Arlen Alexander, George R. Angersbach, Donald Armstrong, Kathleen Mary Askew, Paul Ayres, Brad Ballard, Art Baske, Ed Bayless, Lauren L. Bowler, Gene Butera, John G. Callies, the Campbell-Ewald Co., Chevrolet Div,. Larry Colwell Jr., Mike Cristache, R.R. Donnelley and Sons, Roger Dye, Elliott M. Estes, the F-Car Project Center Staff, Wayne L. Field, Fisher Body Div., George Flaig, Larry Fletcher, Norman G. Fugate, Dr. Suzanne M. Gatchell, Russell F. Gee, General Motors Assembly Div., General Motors Design Staff, General Motors Photographic, Thomas Goad, Ray Green, Stefan Habsburg, Robert J. Haglund, Dick Hanson, Jack Hatfield, John F. Harris, J.W. Herbert, Robert Hill, David R. Holls, Roger E. Hughet, Jack Humbert, John Jackson, Floyd C. Joliet, Charles M. Jordan, Jackie Kiehn, Paul J. King, R.A. Kirkman, Robert H. Knickerbocker, Ralph Kramer, Bill Lawless, P.W. Leistra Jr., Libbey-Owens-Ford, Robert D. Lund, Pete Lupescu, William P. Madigan, Steve Major, F. James McDonald, David S. McIntosh, George A. McLean, Cliff Merriott, Ed Mertz, Norm Milostan, Ronald W. Mitchell, George E. Moon, Thomas G. Morrisey, Lloyd Nedley, Bob Neuharth, Robert L. Norwood, W.R. O'Neil, Jerry P. Palmer, W.H. Percival, V.W. Piggins, Pittsburgh Plate Glass, Pontiac Motor Div., Duane Poole, William L. Porter, Charles L. Potter, Jack Reilly, Rochester Products Div., Jill Rogers, Ed Roland, Don Runkle, Elia Russinoff, Irwin W. Rybicki, F.J. Schaafsma, Jack Schwarz, William S. Schindler, John R. Schinella, William D. Scott, Nettie S. Seabrooks, Orval C. Selders, Bob Shick, Leopold T. Szady, Edward R. Taylor, Roland S. Taylor, A.W. Tholl, Dick Thompson, Charles H. Torner, Kay Ward, Lawrence M. Weathers, D.I. Wenzler, Al Whittemore, Stanley R. Wilen, James J. Williams, Phil Workman, Yenko Chevrolet, Paul Zangerle, Thomas R. Zimmer, and John Zwerner.